to

....

From

....

Most Charisma House Book Group products are available at special quantity discounts for bulk purchase for sales promotions, premiums, fund-raising, and educational needs. For details, write Charisma House Book Group, 600 Rinehart Road, Lake Mary, Florida 32746, or telephone (407) 333-0600.

Take Hold of Your Dream by Jentezen Franklin
Published by Charisma House
Charisma Media/Charisma House Book Group
600 Rinehart Road, Lake Mary, Florida 32746
www.charismahouse.com

Unless otherwise noted, all Scripture quotations are from the King James Version of the Bible.

Scripture quotations marked NAS are from the New American Standard Bible. Copyright © 1960, 1962, 1963, 1968, 1971, 1972, 1973, 1975, 1977, 1995 by the Lockman Foundation. Used by permission. (www.Lockman.org)

Scripture quotations marked NIV are from the Holy Bible, New International Version. Copyright © 1973, 1978, 1984, International Bible Society. Used by permission.

Scripture quotations marked NKJV are from the New King James Version of the Bible. Copyright © 1979, 1980, 1982 by Thomas Nelson, Inc., publishers. Used by permission.

Scripture quotations marked NLT are from the Holy Bible, New Living Translation, copyright © 1996, 2004. Used by permission of Tyndale House Publishers, Inc., Wheaton, IL 60189. All rights reserved.

Scripture quotations marked THE MESSAGE are from *The Message: The Bible in Contemporary English*, copyright © 1993, 1994, 1995, 1996, 2000, 2001, 2002. Used by permission of NavPress Publishing Group.

Cover design by De Wet van Deventer

Visit the author's website at www.jentezenfranklin.org.

International Standard Book Number: 978-1-61638-590-3
Library of Congress Control Number: 2011928390

Previously published by Struik Christian Gifts, an imprint of Struik Christian Media, ISBN 978-1-4153-0892-9.

12 13 14 15 16 — 9 8 7 6 5 4 3 2
Printed in Canada

TAKE HOLD
of Your
DREAM

*Five easy steps to turn
your dreams into reality*

JENTEZEN FRANKLIN

CHARISMA
HOUSE

Contents

Introduction

Who's Been Dumping on Your Dream?

I heard a story about a couple in Southern California who lived in the foothills of the mountains. One day as they were hiking through a canyon, they noticed wild mushrooms growing everywhere. They decided to pick the mushrooms and take them home. They invited some friends over for a "mushroom party." They sautéed the mushrooms, breaded them and fried them. They made mushroom omelets, mushroom salad and mushroom soup. They even concocted some mushroom desserts.

After dinner, as all of the guests were gathered at the table, having a great time, the host went into the kitchen with the leftovers. He had an old, lazy cat, so he decided to feed it with some scraps from the table. The cat gobbled up the mushrooms.

Some time later, the host went back into the kitchen and found the cat lying on the floor, foaming at the mouth and panting for breath. He immediately phoned the veterinarian, who advised the man that he and his dinner guests had better get to the emergency room as soon as possible to have their stomachs pumped. The vet suspected that they had picked poisoned toadstools instead of mushrooms.

After going to the hospital and having their stomachs pumped, the people finally made it back home. They made their way into the kitchen, expecting to see their cat lying lifeless on the floor. Instead, the cat was in the corner of the kitchen with a brand-new litter of kittens!

Imagine that! Have you ever felt like that? What they thought were death pains were, in reality, birth pains! It may look like your dream is foaming at the mouth and panting for its final breath, when in reality you're closer to giving birth to your dream than you've ever been.

If you are discouraged and feel as though your dream is dying, don't give up! Don't give up too soon on your dream. It may be you're just having birth pains, not death pains. It's always too soon to quit.

Keep going. Keep dreaming the dream that God has put into your heart. If it were easy, anyone could do it.

It's Always Too Soon to Quit

It can be the same with you and your life. You can misread the message of your circumstances and thereby miss your destiny. As you read this book, I want to equip you so that won't happen. I want to equip you to believe that you can reach your dream.

When you begin to pursue your dream, somebody will always emerge to try to steal it. Often it will be someone who never had a dream of their own, or if they did, they abandoned it. It could even be a family member who constantly reminds you of what God couldn't or wouldn't do through someone like you.

The question is not can you dream,
but do you have the courage to act on it?

What do you dream about? What has God enabled you to see that does not yet exist? You will never outdream God! Listen: "God can do anything, you know—far more than you could ever imagine or guess or request in your wildest dreams!" (Eph. 3:20, *The Message*).

God loves dreamers. When you dream, you move closer to the way He sees things. In that moment, you rise above your limitations; you move from where you are to where He wants you to be. The question is not can you dream, but do you have the courage to act on it? Is there a dream in your heart? Has life buried it? Have others told you it's too late? Don't you believe it!

Pursue your dream no matter how far-fetched it may seem, for dreams are like children—they're your offspring. Protect them! Feed them! Encourage them to grow, because as long as you have a dream, you'll never be old! I'm talking about a God-given dream that leads to God-honoring results. God has a dream for you, and if you will seek Him, He will reveal it.

My dream is to help you unlock your dreams, and my prayer is that you will step out in faith to claim your destiny.

Chapter 1

Write the Vision

A lot of people talk about having "vision" for their lives, but they don't understand the process or the journey of a vision. They say that God has given them a "dream" of something, but as time goes on, they lose track of it. They don't really know what a dream is supposed to look like.

The enemy does not want you to keep track of your vision. He wants to distract you from it. I love what the verse says in the beginning of the second chapter of the Book of Habakkuk, because it highlights the purpose of a dream or vision, and it also gives some very practical advice on how to handle it:

Then the Lord answered me and said:

"Write the vision

And make it plain on tablets,

That he may run who reads it.

For the vision is yet for an appointed time;

But at the end it will speak, and it will not lie.

Though it tarries, wait for it;

Because it will surely come,

It will not tarry...

The just shall live by his faith."

—Habakkuk 2:2–4, nkjv

As soon as you grasp what your vision is, God wants you to write the vision down so that you can be focused on what He has revealed. He doesn't want you to lose track of it.

The enemy wants to substitute a different vision so that you become diverted and discouraged. But if you have it written down, you can remember what God spoke to your heart and you can go back to that point of reference and remind yourself, "This is what the Lord said." My Bible is marked from one end to the other with things that I've heard the Lord speak to me.

It's good to "make it plain," as the Lord said to Habakkuk, because if you don't make it plain, you won't know where you're going, and you'll be like the man who jumped on a horse and took off going in all directions. He ended up going in circles. Make it as plain as you can. The Lord's way is not complicated.

Beginning With a Burden

Back at the very beginning of the Book of Habakkuk, we read this line: "The burden which the prophet Habakkuk saw" (Hab. 1:1). At first, God will place a burden on your heart.

What does a burden feel like? Habakkuk said three things about his burden. He said, "I felt it. I saw it. And I heard it." Something came over his heart, and he felt it. He saw a need, and God burdened him with it. After a while, God transferred it from being a burden to becoming a vision.

When it changed from a burden to a vision, it became plain. God does not mumble. When God speaks, you don't have to say, "I wonder if I just heard Him." When He speaks, it's not "maybe" or "I hope so." When God speaks, a knowing comes into your spirit, and you have a definite sense. You'll think, "I have just heard from the Lord."

When it becomes plain like that to you, write it down.

When God speaks, a knowing comes into your spirit, and you have a definite sense.

We have no excuse for not knowing God's vision for our lives, because God always has something for each one of us.

The way to find out what He has for you is to be alone with Him. Spend time with Him. Make it possible for Him to take you up a little bit higher, so that He can begin to slip a burden into your heart and put a vision before the eyes of your spirit.

Keeping Your Focus

Besides giving you a vision in the first place, God wants you to focus on Him as you walk it out, because you are going to need His strength to do it. Without His strength along the way, you will not be able to accomplish what God has given you.

A vision is a supernatural thing, and you need to walk it out with supernatural power. That's the same as living by faith, as Habakkuk put it. If you don't keep your focus on God and on what He has told you, and if you don't keep walking by faith the whole time, you stand a very good chance of losing track of your vision.

It is important to keep your focus not only on God, but also on the vision itself. Paul said, "This one thing I do" (Phil. 3:13).

Get a clear idea of what God wants you to do, and get focused on it. Then, hold on and run with it.

Get a clear idea of what God wants you to do, and get focused on it. Then, hold on and run with it. You may pant with desperation sometimes, but don't give up.

4

Paul had a vision that showed him he was supposed to go to Macedonia. It was exciting, the birth of the vision. But when he got there, they beat the daylights out of him and threw him into prison. That could have been the death of his vision right there, but then an angel came and set him free to fulfill the vision. In essence, the angel resurrected his vision. That's the journey a vision will take you through every time—birth, death and resurrection.

One of the most important ways you can tell
if a dream or a vision is from God is that it
will always be bigger than you are.

It Is Bigger Than You

One of the most important ways you can tell if a dream or a vision is from God is that it will always be bigger than you are, and it will always be bigger (and better) than you think.

A vision from God is orchestrated by God Himself. He is always working behind the scenes. He is preparing other people, people you never met before, people you never dreamed of, so that they are ready to catch what you're going to throw and throw what you're going to catch. You may think, "Here I have a vision from God. Now it's all up to me to make it happen." But it's really His vision. It's up to Him to make it happen.

You may have said, "I want to make a million dollars in my business." If you can connect that dream to the harvest, then God can bless it.

You may have said, "I want to be a star athlete, and I want to play in professional sports." If you can tie your dream back to the harvest, then He can bless it.

All you have to do is obey step by step. Your vision will happen as God moves you and, simultaneously, as He moves other people and circumstances. All of these kingdom connections will start to occur. They'll come from every direction. That's not coincidental; it's God.

How Is It Connected to the Harvest?

Not only should you expect your vision from God to be big, but you should also look for how it is connected to the harvest of His kingdom. Joseph had a dream about being in a harvest field (Gen. 37). The harvest portion of your dream may not be quite as obvious to you as it was to him, but look for the connections. How is your dream connected to the harvest?

Harvest means building God's kingdom, building the local church, and increasing the influence of God's kingdom in the world around you.

It's not just a matter of getting what you want...
It's a matter of looking for the harvest connection.

It's not just a matter of getting what you want, which would be a selfish thing. God won't be committed to that. It's a matter of looking for the harvest connection. You see, a God-given dream always has a kingdom purpose.

Because God's ultimate purpose is to bring in the harvest,

you and I need to dream harvest dreams. It's OK to dream of having a better house, a nicer car, a higher standard of living. But at some point, instead of just saying, "Bless me," we need to be able to say, "Lord, use me. Help me fulfill my dream so I can be a blessing to others in Your kingdom."

God's Dreams Will Come to Pass

Remember what the Lord said to Habakkuk? "For the vision is yet for an appointed time; but at the end it will speak, and it will not lie: though it tarry, wait for it; because it will surely come, it will not tarry" (Hab. 2:3). In other words, even though your dream may seem slow to come about, you can know that if a dream comes from God, it will always happen eventually.

A God-given dream always has a kingdom purpose.

You may need to "wait for it" (Habakkuk's words). You may need patience and perseverance. But your patience will be rewarded, because it will come to pass.

When your initial excitement wears off and everything seems to have stalled, don't be surprised. This is normal. There is going to come a time when everything looks like the opposite of what you thought God told you. When it comes (and this may happen more than once), don't give up, don't cave in, don't throw in the towel. It will surely come to pass.

God's visions become reality. God's dreams happen. He may need to go find another dreamer (if you give up), but His dream will happen. You need to stick around long enough to see it happen. You have to be tenacious about your vision.

Take off running with it, hold it close to your chest, and don't stop.

Response Leads to Results

God will never give you the whole thing worked out ahead of time. He just tells you, "Go. I will fill in the details." You have to respond to that somehow. Ideally, you will respond immediately and obediently. God is looking for a spontaneous response from you when He tells you to do something. He doesn't want you to send it off to a committee for a thorough evaluation. He doesn't want you to take it too lightly, to forget about it, or to put it on a shelf. He wants you to do something right away.

The reason so many people are "stuck" where they are and they never go anywhere is that whenever God has told them to do something, they have pulled out their long list of questions before responding in faith. If you wait until every question has been answered before you move, you'll never do anything.

You may not know how something can ever happen, but when God says "Do this!" there's something about an immediate response that impresses Him. The rest of your response involves stepping out and walking by faith.

> If you wait until every question has been answered
> before you move, you'll never do anything.

When God calls you to do something, you have to be willing to go someplace new. Responding to God is going to mean change in your life. Walking with God requires an ongoing, ever-changing experience. One of the sure signs that God is doing something in your life is that change is involved.

Now, most of us are not too fond of change. In fact, we hate it. We go into change kicking and screaming. We prefer our old, familiar landscape and our customary routines. Maybe—just maybe—we become willing to step into something new once we have satisfied ourselves that we know what to expect and if we have worked out all the details ahead of time. But that's not how God works. He just puts you out there in some wilderness, and He makes sure that the only thing you have to hang on to is Him.

God will supply you with the next step as if He is giving you pieces to a puzzle. If you find the place where one piece fits and step forward, He will hand you another one. If you move when He says move, the details will fit themselves in.

How long has it been since you were close enough to God for Him to disturb your schedule and routine? Are you up for the challenge of change? The fulfillment of your destiny lies on the other side of change.

Taking Hold:

- Your dream will begin with a burden of some sort, and that burden will become a vision.
- You'll know your dream is from God if it is bigger than you and if it has to do with the harvest field of the kingdom of God.
- Keep a record of your dream so that you don't forget it. Write it down.
- God's dream will come to pass. Although it may seem to die for a time, God will resurrect it.

Chapter 2

Discovering Your Mission in Life

*T*he purpose of life is to live a life of purpose. God is looking for people to whom He can transfer his passion and dream. Israel's greatest enemies were not the giants without, but the voices within—that voice on the inside that said, "It can't be done. Play it safe." If you're going to be a dreamer, God wants you to take risks! If you dream, it means you expose yourself to ridicule and failure.

Don't be so fearful of what people might say about you that

you abandon your God-given dream. Believe that you can do all things through Christ who strengthens you.

The Birth, Death, and
Resurrection of Your Vision

When you first respond to God as I described in the previous chapter, you are bringing about the birth of your vision. And like everything else in the kingdom of God, a birth is followed by a death and then by a resurrection.

The Purpose of Life Is to Live a Life of Purpose

Every one of God's visions and dreams goes through this process of birth, death and resurrection. God uses that process to sanctify that dream so that when it really does come to pass, it will not be an egotistical thing for you. You will know beyond a shadow of a doubt that God did it, because it used to look so hopeless. He finished what He started.

I guarantee you—if you have a dream, the way you will know it's from God is if you see these three stages: the birth of the vision, the death of the vision and the resurrection of the vision. If you are in the middle of that process right now, don't give up! Whether it's your marriage or business or anything else, ask the Lord to send you some encouragement and a new supply of faith.

Patience Wins the Race

You have to endure patiently. It might take a long time, but victory is achievable. It's like the torch race in the ancient Greek Olympics that was different from other races. In the other races, the winner was the one who crossed the finish line first. But in the torch race, they lit a bunch of torches and handed them out to every runner. They started the race with the fires burning, and the only way you could win the torch race was to finish with your fire still lit. Just because you made it first didn't count until they checked to see if your fire was still burning.

> Just because you made it first
> didn't count until they checked to see
> if your fire was still burning.

I want to be like a winning torch racer. I want to keep moving as fast as I can, but I am not going to lose my fire if I can help it. The important thing is not how quickly I can make it, how quickly my church or my ministry grows, how fast my business grows—it's whether or not I still have the fire of God burning when I cross the finish line. Am I willing to stay around not only for the birth of my vision, but also for its death and the resurrection, which might take years?

The Power of an Unforgettable Dream

The power of an unforgettable dream is that it just keeps going until, one of these days, it is fulfilled. It doesn't matter how many setbacks occur or how many obstacles are thrown in the way. It's never too late. It came from God, and it still belongs to Him. God made the promise, and He has the power to fulfill it.

It's Never Too Late

Amos 3:12 says, "A shepherd who tries to rescue a sheep from a lion's mouth will recover only two legs or a piece of an ear. So it will be for the Israelites in Samaria" (nlt).

This paints a picture: the lion had devoured the lamb, leaving only a leg or two and a piece of an ear. The Scripture says that when the shepherd saw that there was nothing left of that sheep except an ear and a couple of legs, remarkably, he walks over and snatches the ear and the legs from the mouth of the lion. Why? If I were the shepherd, I wouldn't do that. I would see that it's over. My sheep has been devoured. It's finished.

It's never too late. We serve a God of resurrection, and He will resurrect your dream so that you can reach its fulfillment.

But the shepherd—who is a picture of Jesus—saw in that sheep something that was still redeemable. As long as you have an ear to hear and a leg to stand on, it doesn't matter what the enemy has devoured. God can redeem it. It's not in what you've lost; it's in what you have left.

It's never too late. We serve a God of resurrection, and He will resurrect your dream so that you can reach its fulfillment. As long as you still have an ear to hear, even as you're reading this book, He will be speaking to you. Then you can stand on what you've heard.

Nothing is impossible. Believe that you can!

Joseph and You

The story of Joseph is a perfect illustration of the power of a dream. Joseph persisted for years through all kinds of difficulties. For a long time, his dream seemed to have died. He went through all sorts of things. But God kept his dream alive, and He resurrected it. In the end, Joseph's original dream was completely fulfilled. (You can read the story in the Book of Genesis, beginning with chapter 37.)

You and I probably will have to pass the same tests as Joseph did before our dreams will come true. Let's draw out the main steps in the process.

Obtaining Favor

Favor means that God has already prepared things ahead of you so that when you get there, you will walk into them. Favor is the way He makes "all things work together for good" (Rom. 8:28). It means God has called you to the front of the line.

Joseph had favor and everybody knew about it. His coat of many colors represented the favor of his father. That coat stood out! It advertised favor.

It's the same with you and me. When God blesses you real good, it can be hard to conceal it. When God starts blessing you, He blesses you so that you will be seen by others as someone who is highly favored of God.

Joseph's father put that coat on his son to prepare him for his dream. Anytime God begins to favor you and to bless you, it's to prepare you for a dream.

Anytime God begins to favor you and to bless you, it's to prepare you for a dream.

We enjoy a degree of favor from the moment we're saved, but in order to walk into the rest of our destiny, we need to receive more of it. The way it usually works in the kingdom of God is that you have to ask for favor. "Ye have not," James said, "because ye ask not" (James 4:2).

When you open your mouth and ask for favor, God will rain it down on you. So don't put it off! Raise your voice and establish the fact that you are on the favor-receiving end right this minute, even if you just lost your job and you don't know where the next one is coming from.

Declare something like this:

> I am highly favored of the Lord. His favor is preceding me and making a way for me. He is making others look at me with favor. God has decreed it, and He has already sent it. It's like a cloud over me, and I'm just going to announce it. All I have to do is ask, and then I'll get in on the outpouring of favor.

Be sure to notice the connection between fields and favor. Joseph's favored status enabled him to believe his dream about a field with the sheaves of grain bowing down to his sheaf (Gen. 37:5–6). We can find another biblical example of the connection between fields and favor in the story of Ruth. Ruth made a special request that she would be able to work in the field of someone who would show her favor (Ruth 2:2).

You have a field with favor in it too. You may feel that you are supposed to go into the field of medicine or the field of teaching. If you pray before you set foot on your field and you pray to be led to the field of God's choosing, you will receive favor in your harvest field.

Ruth shows us something else, and that is the importance of hanging around other people who carry favor. In her case, it was her mother-in-law, Naomi, who was one of God's chosen people. Ruth had come from Moab. The people of Moab were the opposite of chosen. In fact, they were cursed. But when Ruth decided to stick with Naomi, she started to walk into favor.

If you hang around people who have God's favor on them already, and then if you ask God to guide you to the field of His choosing for your life, you will be able to experience God's faithfulness firsthand.

Dreaming of Harvest

Notice again the setting of Joseph's first dream. It was a harvest field, where the grain was in the process of being harvested and bound into sheaves. I want to reemphasize the idea that your own field needs to be connected to harvest. So, if you have a dream, you can be sure that it's from God if it has something to do with the harvest.

Joseph didn't stop with one harvest dream. He dreamed another dream, and this time it was the sun and moon and stars that were bowing down. This dream was bigger and better than the first one. God's dreams are progressive. Stop thinking that your best days are behind you. Your dream is ahead of you, and it is pointing you forward. It's bigger and better than anything that has happened in your past.

*W*hen you look for
a church, look for one that has
the favor of God on it.
When you get under leadership, look
for leadership that has
the favor of God on it. You won't be
able to go any higher than
the favor you're under.

Stripped and Put Down

Of course, inevitably, if you are walking around displaying God's favor, and if, like Joseph, you happen to tell somebody about the full magnitude of your dream, you will be put down.

So if you have a lot of pressure on you right now and you seem to be seeing more adversity than blessing, I want to tell you that this is not an indication that you should give up. It very well could be an indication that the enemy knows you're closer to having your dream come to pass than you ever have been before. The enemy knows that he needs to conspire against you and attack you and stop you because your dream is for real. You can't quit now!

If God placed that dream in
your heart, and if you don't let go
of it, nobody can stop it.

If God placed that dream in your heart, and if you don't let go of it, nobody can stop it. Nobody's "no" can compete with God's "yes." If God says yes, then it's "yes and amen." If God opens a door, no man can shut it.

So what if people leave you? So what if they say they don't believe you or if they say that God is not with you? Your dream is still intact and moving forward. This is just a test you will have to pass before you get to the fulfillment of it.

So what if you get stripped of the outward expression of blessing and favor? The inward expression of blessing is still there, even though it may be dry as a desert. That is part of the test. When there's no external sign of blessing and no internal sense of blessing, your dream is being tested.

I've heard it said, "The test comes to teach you a lesson." But I never took tests in school to learn my lessons. The teacher would first teach me something and then give me a test. If God is putting you through a test, it is not because He wants to teach you something. It's a sign that He has already taught you something and now you're ready to get through the test.

Remember, the teacher is always silent during the test. Also remember that it's an open-book test! Open God's instruction book called the Bible, and read the instructions.

When you can't hear God, read God.

Maybe your dream is being severely tested and you're trying desperately to put all the pieces together. God's Word to you today is this: Get back into the Word of God. When you can't hear God, read God.

If you'll read God, you'll start hearing God again. When all else fails, read the instructions.

The Return of Favor

If you wait long enough, favor will return. After Joseph's brothers had stripped off his coat of favor, they decided not to kill him, but instead to sell him as a slave. And where did he end up? In the household of Potiphar, the chief bodyguard of the pharaoh of Egypt. That's not what Joseph's brothers had anticipated.

Even though Joseph was still just a teenager with no experience or training, everything that young man did prospered. It was as if he were wearing his coat of favor again, even though now he was dressed in Egyptian clothes.

It will be the same with you. The coat may be missing, but that is a temporary situation. In spite of what you haven't yet received, you are still blessed. It's just a matter of time. Just stand fast—even if you get thrown down again, which is what happened to Joseph. (See Genesis 39:19–20.)

Dream On

I don't need to tell you that being thrown into prison was not part of Joseph's dream plan. You would think that this would have killed Joseph's dream once and for all. In prison, everyone's dreams seemed to be dead, except the dreams of the pharaoh's butler and the pharaoh's baker, each of whom had a literal dream, followed by the important dreams of Pharaoh himself.

If you want to have a God-given dream, you need to get around other dreamers. Dreamers inspire dreams in other people. Joseph's dream is what inspired the butler, the baker and the pharaoh. When they got around him, their dreams began to manifest. Are the people you're in relationship with inspiring your dream?

Dreamers inspire dreams in other people.

Who will help you bring things together first so that you can get to that point? When you are walking out your destiny, two of the kinds of people who need to come into your life are the "bakers" and the "butlers." Who is your baker, and who is your butler? A baker is somebody who pulls it all together. A butler is somebody who opens doors for people.

A baker can take different ingredients—a handful of flour, an egg and a pinch of salt—and make something out of it. He pulls things together and makes something. You may need somebody who mentors you in how to pull it all together.

Then there is the butler, the door opener. He's somebody who's in the right place at the right time for you. He gives you a door you can walk through, an opportunity. The butler turned out to be the one who got Joseph released from prison.

God has butlers, bakers, and pharaohs assigned to your dream. Begin to ask Him to release them in your life.

Joseph's Dream and Your Dream

All of the things that Joseph had to go through apply to you, especially the parts about evil turning into good. The enemy will laugh at you sometimes. But your God will not allow the enemy to assassinate the dream God has given you.

Did you write down the vision? Did you make it plain in the early stages? Then you can keep running with it. If somebody tries to steal it, you can just put your head down and keep running. If it seems to tarry, do not give up on it. If your dream seems to die, tell it to live. Watch God resurrect it. Keep reminding yourself that you can do all things through Christ who strengthens you (Phil. 4:13). Tell yourself that every door that needs to open for you will open for you. Remind yourself that you are not going to wander through life, because your dream has become part of your spirit. It used to be a burden, and you didn't know what it could do, but now you know it's a dream, and it's carrying you!

Taking Hold:

- God is looking for people to whom He can transfer His passion and dream, people to whom He can give a vision and a dream.
- Every one of His visions and dreams goes through a process of birth, death and resurrection. God will not allow the enemy to assassinate your dream. Dreams from God are unforgettable. They will always come to pass, even if it seems to take forever.
- Let Joseph's story remind you of the stages of the journey of your dream. You will see the harvest field, times of favor and disfavor, and the restoration of your dream afterward. You will see how the dreams of others connect with your dream.
- It's not how quickly you get to the fulfillment of your dream; it's how well you finish.

Chapter 3

You Will Come to Vision

The phrase "I will come to vision" comes from a little line in 2 Corinthians 12: "I will come to visions and revelations of the Lord" (v. 1). Can this possibly apply to you and me? Yes, it can—dreams and visions and destiny are not just for exceptional people like Paul.

I may not have the same vision as Paul, but I too will come to the particular vision that is the will of God for my life.

These are the things that God wants me to accomplish. And I will come to a point where I recognize them as being mine, from Him.

Not Goal Setting

Now, I need to make a distinction here. In a lot of places these days, you hear about goal setting. It seems as if all of the "success stories" talk about goal setting. There's nothing wrong with having goals, but a vision is not the same thing. You set up a goal with your carnal human mind. A vision originates with God. It is a spiritual thing. God puts it in your spirit.

When you begin to come to your vision, you can almost hear God saying, "This is My dream and My vision and My destiny for your life." It will always be bigger than what you thought you could ever do or be. It will always be impossible to achieve without the continual help of the Holy Spirit.

But it's not your idea in the first place. It is His.

When you begin to come to your vision,
you can almost hear God saying,
"This is the highest you!"

That's what happened for Paul. Something shifted. After that, he could say affirmatively, "I will come to vision!" His faith suddenly took a quantum leap, and he actually believed God was going to take him someplace he'd never been before. The same thing will happen for you. It's as if your spirit glimpses the reality God has for you, and then it catches its breath. Suddenly you realize that you're about to step out into something that is beyond yourself.

What is the thing you're hoping against hope for? With Paul, he couldn't even tell people about it directly after he reached it, he was so humbled by this experience. It changed him. After that, he walked straighter. He was much more sure of how God saw him. He could share the inspiration with others. He could write in his letter to the Corinthians: "I will come to visions."

He had turned a corner. A lot of the outer details of his life stayed the same. He was still buffeted by circumstances. He still didn't see the complete fulfillment of his dream. But his faith had been ignited as never before.

No matter what you're dealing with right now, you will come to vision. Hell can't stop it; demons can't stop it—you will come to vision!

The way you know that
you're called is that you can't do
anything else and be happy.

The way you know that you're called is that you can't do anything else and be happy. Then you know you're really called! When He calls you to the missionary field, or when He calls you to be an evangelist or to build a corporation, then you cannot get away from it. "For the gifts and calling of God are without repentance" (Rom. 11:29).

Just say, "God, give me Your intentions." Give Him permission to bring you to your vision.

Application

You have to apply to know your vision, the same way you might apply for a job. You can't just float through life and expect your vision to happen to you.

You must believe that all things are possible—even in your own life. You must raise your eyes up off the floor and fix them on Him. Ask Him to give you your vision. Apply for it. Tell Him, "God, I want Your dream." Seek His will today and every day. And when it seems to have been taken away from you, speak life back into your dream.

Don't be passive. Don't be a floater kind of person. Instead, be active. Lay hold of your dream, because having a dream will make you disciplined. It will give you the power you need to look at temptations and say, "No, I know where I'm going, and it's not that direction."

You need a dream to keep you focused and disciplined.

Four Consequences of a Dream

Standing before King Agrippa, the apostle Paul said, "I was not disobedient unto the heavenly vision" (Acts 26:19). Paul was saying, "In spite of the setbacks, in spite of the hardships, I was not disobedient to the heavenly vision."

Paul was not disobedient to his vision from God because along with the vision, God did four things for Paul. When you get a vision from God for your life, He absolutely will do these same four things for you!

The Vision Stops You

On the road to Damascus, the vision stopped Paul. You know the story. In the middle of the day, he's riding his horse, and the Son of God appeared to him as bright as the noonday sun and knocked Paul off his horse. Suddenly, he was stopped.

Something will happen to you when you find God's perfect will, purpose and plan for your life. It will stop you in your tracks. You may be totally happy doing what you're doing, and then, all of a sudden, it just hits you, and instantly everything is changed.

The Vision Sends You

Not only did Paul's vision stop him from what he was doing, but it also sent him to Rome and to other nations to stand before great kings and be a witness for Christ. When you get a real vision from God about your life, it will send you some-place. It will send you to other people. That's one way you can tell the difference between vision and ambition. Vision comes from God, and it will make you help people; ambition comes from your flesh, and it will make you use people.

When God promotes you, His vision is not so you can say, "Look at me," but it is so that you can use your influence to touch other people. A God-given vision will send you to new places and new faces.

The Vision Strengthens You

First, God sent a vision that stopped Paul, and then He sent him. Then, just as important as those two, God gave Paul the strength he needed to carry the vision out—for years and years, through all sorts of setbacks. He will do the same for you so that when adversity comes, when all hell is breaking loose, you will have the strength to get up and keep on going. Only a real vision and a real dream can do that!

A God-breathed vision puts strength right into you. Then you can go on and press on in spite of everything!

A God-breathed vision puts strength
right into you. Then you can go on and
press on in spite of everything!

When Paul said that he was not disobedient to the heavenly vision, what kinds of challenges to his obedience had he faced? Look at this list of potential setbacks and difficult circumstances. God must have sent him more-than-adequate strength to go through more-than-average trials: endless travel over all kinds of terrain on foot and by other difficult and unsafe means, imprisonment, beatings and whippings and stonings, hunger and thirst and poverty. (See the whole long list in 2 Corinthians 11:23–28.)

Yes, he went through all of that and more, but Paul the great apostle thinks of it as the "small print" of his life.

Paul went through all this stuff, and what helped him through it? A great vision. His dream was much bigger than the small print of life. He could think happy because of God's call on his life.

The Vision Stretches You

Paul's dream stretched him. The vision helped him become what he would never have become without it.

It's like the Olympics. When those athletes stand and get their gold medals, they'll often break down crying. They're not crying over that moment of getting the medal around their necks; they're thinking about all the stuff they had to go through to get there. That's what praise is. You don't just praise Him because you feel good right now. But real, anointed praise is when you remember what you came through.

*A*re you in a job that's
stretching you? Or are you just
in a place of contentment and at ease?
"Woe to them that are at ease
in Zion" (Amos 6:1).
Paul's dream stretched him;
the dream enlarged him. The God-given
vision helped him become what he would
never have become without it.

> Real, anointed praise is when you
> remember what you came through.

The vision God gives you will stretch you. Studies show that the average person only uses five per cent of his or her mental ability. Many people do not ever put themselves in situations that force them to stretch their faith, talent or resources. A rubber band is not effective unless it's stretched. In fact, you could say that a rubber band never fulfills its purpose until it's stretched.

The same is true with us. What's stretching you right now? Most people try to avoid stretching. That's why God often has to bring motivation of some kind before we will stretch. We won't do it naturally.

Have you ever had God push you into something you would have never voluntarily jumped into? Success is facing the challenges of life and not shrinking back from them. Every person God has ever used had to stretch.

> Success is facing the challenges of life
> and not shrinking back from them.

Most people are vulnerable when they are stretching. Just as a rubber band is more likely to snap when it's stretched, the same is true when you stretch to reach your God-given vision.

Remember that every person who has ever stretched has

been tempted to cease stretching because they're discouraged. They need to get around others who will encourage them. Most people need affirmation when they're stretching. The most important time to encourage people is when they're taking a risk.

Believe in Yourself

Before you can discover what God has called you to do or you reach your full potential, you have to find a lasting basis on which to build your self-worth. Just as your beliefs can move you forward, your shadow beliefs can hold you back. What are shadow beliefs? That's the committee in your head that tells you that you're not worthy or that you'll never make it.

What are your shadow beliefs? Today, I challenge you to bring them out into the light and expose them to God's Word. Don't let them control you or decide your future. You can't speak death over your dreams and expect to see them come to life.

You can't speak death over your dreams
and expect to see them come to life.

Paul says, "He chose us in Him before the foundation of the world" (Eph. 1:4, nkjv). Imagine, you're called by God and handcrafted for a specific purpose at precisely this time and in precisely this location! Wow!

You came pre-cut to fill a particular place that nobody else could. So stop trying to be like somebody else! If you give up being who you are in order to become like them, you'll end up being somebody God doesn't need one more of. Stop doubting yourself or competing with others. Nobody can take what God has reserved for you!

Today you have a choice; either let others determine your worth, or let God.

Today you have a choice; either let others
determine your worth, or let God.

In Genesis 1:31 we read, "Then God saw everything that He had made, and indeed it was very good" (nkjv). Before you were born, God saw you. He knew the specific purpose you were designed to fulfill, so He provided you with the gifts you would need. Then, He looked at you and said, "Very good."

Can you say that too about yourself? It's important that you can, because others will only treat you according to how you treat yourself. If you don't like the way people respond to you, stop and ask yourself, "What's the message I'm sending?" In order to be treated well, you have to send a message that says, "I'm somebody because God made me somebody."

We're talking here about inner strength that makes you attractive when you walk into a room and causes others to say, "Who's that?" They're not asking because of your physical appearance, but because your presence has impact. This is not pride; it's just healthy self-esteem based on God's opinion of you. It's what I call God-esteem! When you have it, it affects the way you talk to others, apply for a job, perform a ministry or even how you pray. That's right; if you think you have no value, you'll pray with less faith and conclude that the promises of God are for everybody but you.

Appreciate who God made you to be,
and develop what He gave you.

Appreciate who God made you to be, and develop what He gave you. Stop wishing you were somebody else. You have a unique blend of gifts and talents. You have a special destiny on Earth.

Gideon is an example of somebody who wasn't exactly looking to be stretched or to be used by God. Then, along came God's angel, saying, "You are a mighty man of valor!" (See Judges 6:12.) Gideon did not feel like a mighty man of valor, but God had sent the angel to help him see himself that way.

The story goes on to tell how he assembled his army. Thirty-two thousand Israelites showed up to fight the Midianite army. What did God decide to do? He decided to make the army smaller. Anytime God reduces you numerically, it's to drive you back to your source. There's no greater or safer place to be than right in the center of God's will, even if that place seems to be a place of disadvantage.

> There's no greater or safer place to be than right in the center of God's will.

Gideon obeyed when God told him to bring the men down to the water to drink. And he watched how they drank. The ones who used their hands to scoop up the water were the ones God would use to bring about the victory. Why scooping? I think it's because the men who used their hands to scoop up the water had to have empty hands. They had to lay aside their weapons in order to scoop the water. It's as if God were saying, "Come to Me with empty hands. Put down your carnal weapons. I'm not going to use whatever you have been depending on to win this battle."

Besides that, the ones who scooped the water ended up with clean hands. Clean hands represent a level of consecration and holiness that is required when God wants to use you.

Finally, Gideon came to the realization God had reduced his numbers so that he would understand that numbers were never where his strength lay in the first place.

God was his refuge. God was his strength. God alone held the victory in His mighty hand. Gideon's weakness would not be exploited by the enemy. Instead, it would be used by the Lord of hosts to display His magnificent power.

If you don't respond to God's dream for your life, then the enemy wins. If he can make you think you misheard God, maybe he can still prevail. I want to tell you that you are more important than you think you are. Important people do important things. Believe that you can. Build that business, get that degree, launch that ministry, birth that dream.

The Devil's Worst Nightmare

Then what did God tell Gideon to do? He said, "I want you to go and to hear what's going on in the enemy camp." This was a strange instruction. In order to make it possible for Gideon to have enough confidence, God was sending him to hear what his enemies were saying about him. He wanted him to see himself through God's eyes and through the enemy's eyes. If you can see yourself through the enemy's eyes, your confidence will increase.

> The devil's worst nightmare is
> that you and I are going to wake up and
> recognize our authority in Christ.

The devil's worst nightmare is that you and I are going to wake up and recognize our authority in Christ. When you and I discover what our purpose is and how God wants us to approach the battle for victory, we'll know already that we have won, and that will make the devil worried.

The devil's worst nightmare is that you will look beyond the earthly view and see through the eyes of heaven, as Gideon did when he heard what was taking place in the enemy's camp.

The devil's worst nightmare is that you and I will get an understanding of what they're saying in the enemy's camp right now about us. When Gideon heard how fearful his enemy was of him, it boosted his faith to a place where he could say, "I believe that I can do anything." And guess what. As a man thinks, so is he (Prov. 23:7).

I want to tell you that you are more important than you think you are. Important people do important things. Believe that you can. If you can believe it, you can be it.

Don't Quit

This is no time to back up. This is no time to be discouraged. This is a time to say, "God, show me who I really am in You and what I'm capable of."

Gideon led his puny army into battle with 300 men against 250,000, and all they had were a trumpet and breakable pitchers that held a candle of fire. When Gideon said, "Break the jars," those torches flared up. The enemy camp flew into a panic, and they started killing everything in sight—which was each other!

You see, the breaking of the glass pitchers represents a willingness to be broken so that God's light can shine forth. His dream for your life can be fulfilled, even in the face of insurmountable odds. Can God break you and you'll still trust Him enough to pick up the trumpet of praise and glorify Him?

Then you will come to vision. You will believe that you can achieve it. You will take hold of the power of your dream, the destiny that God poured into your spirit when He created you.

Taking Hold:

- God is the giver of visions. Ask Him for yours.
- Visions do four things: they stop you, send you, strengthen you, and stretch you.
- Let Gideon's story remind you about three things: how God sees you, the importance of obedience, and the power of brokenness.
- Remember—the enemy should be the one having nightmares, not you!

Chapter 4

Take Hold of Your Dream

*F*inding out God's will for your life shouldn't depend on "luck" or "fate." And regardless of how your life has treated you, His will for you isn't to give up on you and throw you in the trash. He's not limited by your life circumstances. After all, this is the same God who took nothing and made it into something—this whole big world! He can, and will, do the same thing with your life, even if you think your life is just a big zero.

You have hope, Mr. or Ms. Zero, if you are connected to Jehovah God, because He specializes in taking nothing and nobody and making something beautiful out of it.

Here's why:

> The race is not to the swift,
> Nor the battle to the strong,
> Nor bread to the wise,
> Nor riches to men of understanding,
> Nor favor to men of skill;
> But *time and chance happen to them all.*
> For man also does not know his time:
> *Like fish taken in a cruel net,*
> *Like birds caught in a snare,*
> *So the sons of men are snared in an evil time,*
> When it falls suddenly upon them.
>
> —*Ecclesiastes 9:11–12, emphasis mine*

"Time and chance happen to them all." Another way of saying it is this: God gives everybody a shot at destiny. He created you for something. He didn't create you just to take up space.

Colliding With Your Destiny

You are not an accident. I don't care if you came from an illegitimate birth. No seed and egg can come together and come to full-term life unless God gives life. Nobody is a loser. Every single life has a destiny. God wants each of us to collide with our destiny.

There's a promise and a warning in these words. The promise is that every one of us has a God-ordained destiny. The warning is that you can miss your destiny when the right moment comes if you are entangled in something you have no business being involved in.

Your destiny is connected to a specific, and "evil," time. "For man also does not know his time: like fish taken in a cruel net, like birds caught in a snare, so the sons of men are snared in an evil time" (Eccles. 9:12). God's warning to you is not to be distracted or mixed up in Satan's traps when you are colliding with destiny or you could miss your moment forever.

Satan tries to throw over you
every net he can lay his hands on.

A net is anything that confines and controls you, anything that holds you back from moving on with God. It may be a net of addiction, alcohol or drugs, or a net of offense and unforgiveness. Satan becomes active in your life when he sees that you are about to take hold of your destiny.

"The chance and the time" is already preordained. It's ready for each and every person. But if you're tied up in a net of sin and bondage and bitterness, it will keep you back.

Andrew was involved with his fishing nets when Jesus walked up to him and said two words: "Follow Me." (See Matthew 4:18–20.) Andrew had never seen Him before. Jesus didn't wait for an answer. He didn't give him much time to think. He just said, "Follow Me." And Andrew dropped his nets and followed Him. What would have happened if he had been tangled up in his nets?

Andrew did not miss his collision with destiny. When his destiny came knocking, he didn't keep his hands in his nets. He grabbed hold of his future and became one of Jesus' disciples. The whole kingdom of God was wrapped up in that moment.

What nets are you tangled up in that could potentially stop you from doing what God has designed for you to do? Drop the net and follow Jesus. This is your season for a collision with destiny.

Six Stages to Every Dream

I have identified six stages in the process of how your dream or vision will unfold:

1. I thought it.
2. I caught it.
3. I bought it.

4. I sought it.

5. I got it.

6. I taught it.

I Thought It

This first stage may be just a thought, something that doesn't mean much to the people around you, but to you it's like a revelation. It just won't let you go.

You turn that thought over and over in your mind. "Man, could I really do that? I could do that! I can see myself doing that. It could really happen."

I Caught It

You can't stay at the first stage forever. In fact, if you turn that thought over in your mind enough, it's almost inevitable that you will catch hold of it and begin to talk to other people about it.

Now that you're talking about it, you've "caught" it. You're actually looking into it. You've gone beyond thinking about it.

These two stages may sound familiar. Most people get this far. But too often, somewhere between stage two and stage three, their dream dies.

I Bought It

This is where you have to pay the price. That's the stage beyond talk. Now you have to put it on the line. You have to buy into the dream and take a little risk. You step out on your idea to see if it's strong enough to hold up.

You believe that with God, all things are possible. You begin to pay the price in terms of education and in terms of equipping yourself for fulfilling your dream. You do whatever you have to do.

I Sought It

After you buy into your dream and put some sweat equity into it, then you really get committed. Now nobody can talk you out of it. You can't think of anything else.

I Got It

Now you're there! You grab hold of the whole prize! You've paid the price, and you've walked the walk. And you're glad you did.

I Taught It

There is no success without a successor. Paul had Timothy. Elijah had Elisha. Moses had Joshua. Who are you mentoring, and who is mentoring you?

Taking Hold:

- God created you for something. You have a destiny, and He wants you to know what it is and to take hold of it.
- Most often, you will discover your destiny in six stages: "I thought it, I caught it, I bought it, I sought it, I got it, and I taught it."
- Once you've grabbed hold of your dream, hang on to it in spite of the doubts and difficulties that beset you. Disentangle yourself from whatever holds you back.
- Trust God all the way. Keep your focus on Him. He will make a way for your dream to come true.

Chapter 5

Unfolding Your Dream

I've always had a desire to do something for God. One way it showed was with music. When I was eight or nine years old, I got some empty shoeboxes and I made myself some drumsticks out of pieces of old coat hangers. I would beat my "drums" to the tune of whatever music was playing.

One day my daddy walked in and said, "Since you want to play the drums that bad, I'm going to buy you a drum set." He did, and he moved them into his church. We didn't have a drummer in our church, and I didn't really know how to play. But I had a desire to play the drums for God, and I did.

Then, a few years later, I went to my mom and said, "Mom, I heard a saxophone on a record, and I want to play one." She bought me a saxophone. I don't know why, but I became obsessed with playing the saxophone. It would prove to be a major part of my life.

It Begins With Desire

The point I'm trying to make is that it doesn't begin with talent; it begins with desire. Then, one thing can lead to another. You have to have the desire first or you won't do anything. You have to want it. There's no substitute for desire.

There's always something to hold you back if you let it. There's always an excuse you can give as to why you can't do what God has called you to do. But if you have desire, you can say, with Paul, "None of these things move me."

What are the things that didn't move Paul? It was all those things he listed in 2 Corinthians 11: beatings and stonings and all kinds of hardship and dangers. The apostle Paul was not deterred by the fact that he was not tall and handsome, or that he was not Mr Personality. Apparently, the way he came across to people was weak and contemptible (2 Cor. 10:10).

But he pressed on past all these things, because he had the desire. He didn't make excuses.

No Excuses

You were born with an assignment. Don't die until you've fulfilled it. Your God-given assignment will always tug at your heart and lead you to your highest fulfillment. Your assignment will unlock your compassion and creativity.

Don't let your weakness or feelings undermine your desire. Instead, fan the flames of your desire. It's one of the most important parts of responding to God's vision for your life.

Desire Plus Passion Equals Power

Have you ever wondered if there was one quality, one accomplishment in your life that can excite God more than any other? One thing that can make one person succeed where another fails? One thing that can infuse your life with power and purpose?

Well, there is, and it is not background, giftedness or good looks. It is passion. God loves a person of passion. He will pass up the crowd for the person whose heart is burning with passion, zeal, desire and holy fire.

God will pass up the
crowd for the person whose
heart is burning with passion,
zeal, desire and holy fire.

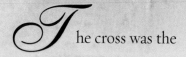

The cross was the "love chamber" of the New Testament. It is where He gave His body to His bride and He said, "I was wounded for your transgressions." (See Isaiah 53:5.)

We've all known people who were quiet, laid back and medio-cre until you touch that one thing they're passionate about, and suddenly they come alive. They rise out of obscurity, no longer wallflowers, but more like heat-seeking missiles.

Passion will take you places and cause you to do things you would never do without it. The key to unleashing God's power is a preceding, overriding passion for Him. There must be passion to ignite the release of His explosive power.

When God sees passion in people, He releases His power through them. I encourage you to follow the example of passionate people such as Elijah, the twelve disciples, and Jesus Himself. Then, apply these principles to your life. When you do, you will see a life-transforming spirit of power and victory take up residence in your soul.

Jesus, a Portrait of Passion

It was "after his passion" (Acts 1:3) that Jesus first demonstrated the power available through His death on the cross. The greatest display of human power ever on the earth was the resurrection of Jesus Christ. No other demonstration of might and victory can come near to that which Jesus displayed in Jerusalem the third day after He was crucified. He defeated death and the grave.

Now, the passion reference of Acts 1:3 refers to the suffering that Christ endured at the crucifixion. But other definitions for passion include "strong feeling," "an abandoned display of emotion," "boundless enthusiasm," and "love." I believe these words apply to Acts 1:3 as well. Because of the pain Christ endured on the cross, we can see His "passion of love" for us.

The reason for the passion of Christ
was His passion for you and me.

The reason for the passion of Christ was His passion for you and me. His death was a demonstration of the unconditional love He has for us. His focus was on us, and that passion is what ultimately led to the power of the cross. This is the power that you and I have access to. It is power for salvation, healing, provisions, relationships, guidance, and so much more.

Elijah—a Man of Fervor

If ever there was a man of passion and power, it was Elijah. Elijah was passionate about his faith, about his God and about the power available to believers. Elijah's passion never failed to bring results.

Passion produces power! The Bible says that this prophet had so much power with God that he prayed both drought and fire down from heaven (1 Kings 17–18). Elijah's passion produced power to revive a dead boy (1 Kings 17:22), outrun a chariot (1 Kings 18:46), and part water (2 Kings 2:8). He was even fed by angels (1 Kings 19:5). Then, rather than leaving this world in the traditional manner, he "went up by a whirlwind into heaven" on a chariot of fire (2 Kings 2:11). Now, that is what I call power. And power always follows passion.

A Woman With Determination

In chapter 5 of the Book of Mark the woman with the issue of blood had such passion and determination that she overcame what seemed to be illogical. Logic said, "There are too many people around Jesus. You cannot get through that crowd." Logic said, "You are ceremonially unclean and cannot go near Christ."

But her passion said, "No matter what my situation, I can get to Jesus. And no matter what my need, He will make it right."

Yes, there were challenges and obstacles to overcome, but this woman wanted her healing more than anything. Mere obstacles would not stand between her and her vision. She had an unrelenting determination—a passionate focus on Jesus Christ.

You won't stumble into your healing;
you have to pursue it.

The indiscriminate, casual worshiper who touches Christ will not receive His power. You have to have a passionate determination to see your need met. You won't stumble into your healing; you have to pursue it.

And here's a bonus effect. If you look in Matthew 14, you will see that this woman opened up a new spiritual dimension of possibilities for others because of her faith. By using her passion, she broke into a whole new dimension of the anointing through the Spirit of God; an anointing that people did not realize existed. And once she broke through with her passion, others began to get their breakthroughs, using the dimension that she opened up.

"Soon people were bringing all their sick to be healed. They begged him to let the sick touch at least the fringe of his robe, and all who touched him were healed" (Matt. 14:35–36, nlt).

God wants to open up new dimensions of worship, new dimensions of power for believers. But He must have people with passionate determination who can release this power.

Your Turn to Change the World

Just as God chose His twelve disciples, He is choosing you today. He is calling you to change the world through the passion and purpose He has placed within you. Get hold of that passion, and nothing will be impossible. Your faith can move your mountain (Matt. 17:20; 1 Cor. 13:2), but your fear can create one.

Out of billions of people, Jesus chose twelve men to be the building blocks of the kingdom of God on Earth. It's really an amazing thing. He did not choose them because of what they were to start with. He chose them because of what He knew they could become through His mighty power infused with their passion. God wants us to be passionate about our needs, but He also wants us to be compassionate about others. He has given us a mission to go out into the world to share His hope and love.

> Your faith can move your mountain,
> but your fear can create one.

The disciples were in the Upper Room for ten days, praying, and nothing happened. Sometimes you go through seasons when you're living in the land of nothing and the only thing that will get you through that nothing is passion.

When Elijah was believing for rain, six times he sent his servant to see what was coming on the horizon. Each time he would ask, "Are there any clouds?" Six times his servant's answer was, "Nothing." On that seventh trip to check for clouds, Elijah's servant saw a cloud on the horizon. Elijah's miracle was on its way! (See 1 Kings 18:45.)

For twelve years, the woman with the issue of blood sought her healing and saw no results. Then, she received her miraculous healing instantly—it only took one touch.

Don't be afraid of failure. Keep your fire of passion burning deep inside. Don't water down your passion based on the circumstances around you. The disciples were persistent and were rewarded with the power of the Holy Spirit.

When you pursue your God-given purpose with a passion, He will anoint you with the power to fulfill it. God's Word is your shield of protection against demons and devils. God's Word is your sword of the Spirit that drives the enemy back. You need to be passionate and desire His Word more than you desire money or pleasure; desire it more than anything. I want to encourage you today to pray for guidance, seek God's will for your life, and study His Word. Your passion will grow and give you the tools you need to accomplish your God-given purpose.

Ask for guidance, seek God's will,
study His Word, and your passion
and your power will grow.

God is looking for people who won't lose their passion no matter what the trial or circumstance. Where is your passion? Where is your compassion? Your relationship with your heavenly Father should be one of passion and fervor. He should be your focus, your desire, the overwhelming love of your life. If you remember this key, you will never lack His power.

*P*assionate people are willing to take risks and try new things… Yes, some met with shocking deaths, but they did something incredible with their lives because of the passion that burned within them.

> When you are down to nothing,
> God is up to something!

This power, born of passion, is what God will use to unleash your divine destiny. You have a God-given purpose, a calling on your life. The passion deep inside you is waiting to be released. God has made a provision of power for you to move forward to achieve that mission. Just tap into the passion of your heart, and remember that passion produces power!

Passion costs you something. It costs to love, to feel, to care, and when Christ hung on that cross, He was saying, "When you look at the cross, don't just see pain, but see My passion for you."

My prayer is that as He gave His body for you, you would give your body back to Him as a living sacrifice, holy and acceptable to God.

Taking Hold:

- Unfolding your dream starts with desire. Desire enables you to persist, even when your circumstances get difficult.
- Besides desire, you need passion. Find your passion and follow it. Remember, power follows passion.
- When you are down to nothing, God is up to something!
- If you follow the example of Jesus, Elijah, the twelve disciples, and many others who have gone before you, you too can be a world changer.

Chapter 6

Making Assets of Your Liabilities

*Z*acchaeus's liability was that he was short. When he heard that Jesus was at the edge of town, he wanted a chance to see Him. Jesus would be walking through town on the main street. People were swarming into the street. But Zack knew that if he just walked out there, he'd only see the backs of the people in front of him. So, he got an idea. He climbed a sycamore tree.

He didn't expect Jesus to notice him. Out of the hundreds

and hundreds of people who lined the streets that day, Jesus chose him to speak to directly. He looked right at him and said, "Zacchaeus, make haste and come down, for today I must stay at your house" (Luke 19:5, nkjv). Zacchaeus's whole life changed. He had met his Savior face to face.

It happened because of, not in spite of, his liability. If he hadn't been so short, he wouldn't have climbed that tree.

Liabilities Become Launching Pads

What is your greatest liability? Whatever you have as a liability could turn out to be your greatest asset if it drives you "up a tree" and causes you to see Jesus. If your liability makes you desperate, it can make you willing to do what others aren't willing to do. You can undertake extreme measures to see Him, and if you're that interested in seeing Jesus, you will see Him not only at a distance, but also up close. He will invite Himself to your house. It will change your life.

Whatever you have as a liability could
turn out to be your greatest asset.

When I was a teenager, I got really sick. Those were some of the darkest days of my life. I went through the dark season for over a year, and it eventually started driving me up a tree. I kept saying, "God, when are You going to heal me? When is this going to be over?" And He would say nothing—nothing but silence. So I began to devour the Bible.

I learned a lot about Him. Out of a dark season like that, you learn things you cannot learn unless you're a "tree person." You learn things you would never learn if your life had been normal and average.

One of the main things I learned was that if God trusts you with a severe trial, it's only because He wants to invite Himself to your house. He has something for you that will come right out of your bad situation. Your greatest liability, the thing that makes you shake your fist at heaven, could become the intimacy point between you and Jesus.

Sometimes you have to go through seasons when you're living in God's "nothing." It's so you will seek Him with passionate desperation. When you're down to nothing, God really is up to something!

Your Problem Is the Key to Your Promotion

Look at David and Goliath. Without Goliath, we would never have heard of David. David could have just continued tending sheep out in the fields if God hadn't sent Goliath. In order to become King David, he had to face Goliath. His problem (Goliath) was the key to his promotion (becoming king).

Can you figure out what your Goliath is? What's your biggest obstacle or problem? It may just be the key to your promotion.

In order for you to step into your destiny, you will need to face down your Goliath-sized problem in God's unbeatable strength. Believing that you can do it is more than half of your battle.

The Lepers' Liabilities

Do you see how important our liabilities can be? Without them, most of us would just settle for the status quo. We'd never exert ourselves to grab hold of God's provision for our lives.

It reminds me of another story in the Bible, the story of the four lepers who lived outside the city wall at Samaria. (See 2 Kings 6:24–7:20.) They had to live on the outside of the walls because they were contaminated and contagious with leprosy. People would throw food scraps over the wall to those four guys, and they would eat the scraps while sitting in the dirt. I believe those lepers would have sat there for years, content with the scraps, if they hadn't been thrown into a major crisis.

The king of Syria besieged the city, and the people began to starve to death. Needless to say, no more scraps came over the wall for the poor lepers.

Finally, the lepers were so desperate that they decided to go into the enemy's camp. If they got killed, what difference would it make? They were going to die anyway.

See, a famine will help you make a "destiny decision." They needed to be motivated to leave behind the land of famine and walk into the place of plenty.

And when they got to the edge of the camp, what did they find? Nobody. Those Syrians had thought they heard the sound of an army coming. They had left everything—food, clothing, everything—and they had fled.

> The real problem has always
> been the battles inside our
> own minds and hearts.

Those lepers expected to face a barrage of arrows, but instead the bigger foe turned out to be the fear inside them. It's the same with you and me. The circumstances have never been our real problem. God is always greater than anything out there. The real problem has always been the battles inside our own minds and hearts.

It didn't take long before they realized that they should tell the starving people inside the city that the siege was over. It was a miracle. The city was saved. And it would not have happened if the lepers' liability had not driven them to take a big risk. Their liability had become their greatest asset.

Worship on the Partial

Most of the time, our liabilities aren't physical ones. Even when we have a physical problem like the lepers did, sometimes it seems like our biggest two liabilities are lack of faith and lack of perseverance. It can sometimes take years before we see results. We need to hold on to our vision through all sorts of setbacks, and we need to believe that our God is more than able to carry us through. He will every time, if we hang on to Him.

One of the best ways to hang on to God is by worshiping and praising Him, regardless of what your circumstances look like. When Zerubbabel and Nehemiah returned from Babylon to Jerusalem to rebuild the walls of Jerusalem, they started, of course, with the foundation. It was hard, hard work, clearing rubble and moving massive slabs of rock. Each day was difficult, but each day counted, because they'd get a little more done. (See Nehemiah 7.)

We need to hold on to our vision
through all sorts of setbacks.

After a while, they finished the foundation. They hadn't yet built the walls. They hadn't yet set up the curtains and the gold and the altars. They had laid only the foundation. You know what a foundation looks like: it's just the shape of the future building, and there's still a lot of work to do.

At that point, the people took a break. And what did they do? The Book of Ezra says this:

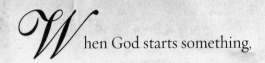

*W*hen God starts something,

He always finishes it.

That's something to praise Him for!

Worship cannot wait.

> And all the people shouted with a great shout, when they praised the Lord, because the foundation of the house of the Lord was laid.
>
> —*Ezra 3:11*

The people made so much noise shouting and worshipping that the noise could be heard "afar off" (Ezra 3:13). Wasn't it a little premature to start a worship service?

No, not at all. The worship itself probably helped the work to proceed successfully. You see, they were worshiping "on the partial." In faith, they were seeing the completed temple. They were praising God for what they had achieved already and putting their trust in Him that it would be completed as planned.

If you can learn to worship "on the partial"—when you don't yet have it all—you will have learned how to walk your vision through to completion. You will be expressing your faith in a God who is able to see you through to the end. When God starts something, He always finishes it.

> When God starts something,
> He always finishes it.

Many of us think we have to wait for our complete victory to happen before we can open our mouths and our hearts in full worship. But I'm telling you that one way to stir up your faith and joy and energy is to begin to worship on the partial. The deal is this: "The joy of the Lord is your strength" (Neh. 8:10). If you lose your joy, then you lose your strength. If you lose your strength, you lose your power to resist the enemy. If you lose the power to resist the enemy, he will have you for lunch.

But if you can worship God, even when all you have in front of you are the foundation stones, the joy of the Lord will fill your heart, and you will not find it so difficult to resist the enemy.

The enemy wants you to get depressed. Satan wants you to throw in the towel.

The antidote is simple—it's worship and praise. Ask yourself the question: Is my God able? Of course, you know the answer. He's able to finish what He starts, and He's able to keep you in there. So, praise Him when the fulfillment of your vision is only partial.

The Four Horns

In the Bible, horns are a symbol or a type of power. In the Book of Zechariah, there is a prophetic word about four horns. (See Zechariah 1:17–21.) These four horns represented four powerful nations that came against the city of Jerusalem right after God had promised prosperity and comfort to the people so they could "spread abroad" His goodness. As soon as God decreed prosperity, these four horns of resistance rose up to hold down God's people.

God has decreed a word over you. He has spoken prosperity over you. I'm talking about prospering in the dream that God has given you to spread it further, to do more and to enlarge your territory. But that doesn't mean that horns will not come to resist the prosperity of God from breaking forth and spreading abroad in your life.

God has spoken prosperity over you.

Zechariah also saw four carpenters. These four carpenters were coming to build up what the four horns would tear down. Jesus was the Son of a carpenter. Just when the horns of the enemy come to press you down and defeat you, God will send the Spirit of the Carpenter to build you back up, to lift you up, to encourage you and to tell you, "The joy of the Lord is your strength."

These four horns don't have names in the Bible, but I have given them names, picking out four ways that Satan tries to hold down God's people:

The Horn of Lack

The first horn represents lack. The horn of lack says, "This is the level that you will operate on for the rest of your life. You're stuck here."

You can get used to a life of lack, but as soon as you start to lift your head up and say, "I'm going to rise to another level so I can do more for God and for my family and for the kingdom," that horn of lack will show up and try to keep you in the same territory that you're used to. Sometimes, "lack" has been keeping you down for so long, even for generations, that you don't realize what it is. You can grow accustomed to a lack of joy, a lack of love in your marriage, a lack of confidence, a lack of peace, or a lack of finances. The horn of lack tries to convince you that God will bless some, but He'll never bless you.

The horn of lack tries to convince you that God will bless some, but He'll never bless you.

In your own life, has a spirit of lack dug itself into you like the point of a horn? Why don't you just say this: "In the name of Jesus, you horn of lack, you are not legal in my life. I serve a God of superabundance. I serve a God who says, 'You shall have good success' (Josh. 1:8). I'm not going to listen to the negative voices anymore."

The Horn of Limitation

The second horn is called the horn of limitation. When you are being held down by the horn of limitation, you know that the power and the blessings of God are real. But you think, "It's not for me." The horn of limitation puts a ceiling over you.

It tells you that you can succeed to a certain degree, but then you will peak and you won't be able to go any higher.

We have had limitations imposed on us. We accept them and we believe them, even when we have long since "outgrown" them.

Tell yourself that you're not the
person you used to be and that your old
limits don't apply to you anymore.

You must determine to push down those limitations. Hear the voice of the Holy Spirit calling you to go a little further, do a little more. Use your faith, and expand beyond the limitations.

Tell yourself that you're not the person you used to be and that your old limits don't apply to you anymore. The Spirit of the Carpenter wants to begin to build you up in your confidence and faith enough to make you free from the limitations that have held you back. Let the Carpenter come and show you how free and strong you really are. Let Him break off your limitations.

The enemy wants you to stay in your limitation. He wants you to put your head down and go into a foxhole because your life is difficult. Just tell that spirit of limitation, "Spirit of limitation, you're not going to hold me down. I'm getting up right now." Don't reinforce those old limitations anymore.

The Horn of Hindrance

In the Book of 1 Thessalonians, Paul named the evil spirit of the third horn. "I desire to come to you, but Satan has hindered me." (See 1 Thessalonians 2:18.)

This hindering spirit gets in front of you and blocks you. It keeps you from making progress.

But in the Spirit of the Carpenter you can say, "Horn of hindrance, you can buffet me. You can try to hinder me. You can delay me. But you cannot destroy me. And you can't stop me. You can knock me down, but 'the righteous will get up seven times.'" (See Proverbs 24:16.)

Let the Carpenter hammer on the third horn until it no longer hinders you.

The Devouring Horn

Now, after you've prevailed against the resistance that gets in front of you to try to hinder you and limit you, another one will get behind you. This one appears in Malachi 3:11.

When you think you've finally gotten your breakthrough and you are starting to see some victories in the harvest, if you don't watch out, this devouring horn will begin to steal the fruitfulness that God has given you.

At first, you may not know what's going on. But when you realize what's happening, you can bind that horn up just like you did the other ones in the authority and strength of the Spirit of the Carpenter.

Right now, open your mouth and confess that God is able to save you; He's able to bring you through in one piece; He's able to do far more abundantly than all you can ask or think (Eph. 3:20).

Worship Him. Let your faith rise. Turn those liabilities of yours into assets, and "press on toward the goal for the prize of the upward call of God in Christ Jesus" (Phil. 3:14, nas).

Taking Hold:

- Your seemingly insurmountable problems can become launching platforms for your faith.
- Sometimes you must go through seasons when you're living in "God's nothing" so you will seek Him with passionate desperation.
- Make a positive confession. Open your mouth with praise; confess that your God is able. He is!
- With God's help, you can prevail over the "four horns" that will try to tear you down: the spirit of lack, the spirit of limitation, the spirit of hindrance, and the devouring spirit.

Chapter 7

Living in the Faith Zone

*C*huck Yeager was the World War II hero who first broke the sound barrier. Everybody who had tried it before had gotten to a certain speed, and the plane had started to shake so violently that it seemed as if the plane would disintegrate. Some planes did disintegrate, and the pilots died. But Yeager wanted to try anyway. He said, "At seven hundred miles an hour, the plane began to rattle and shake violently." But then he broke through into "a great calm." He had done it.

That's how it is when you're about to get a breakthrough. Everything around you starts shaking and falling apart. Everything goes crazy. You might be in pain. You feel as if your whole world is falling to pieces. But that's not an indication that you're going to crash. As if God would drop something He had started! As if He would let you crash and burn!

Breakout Comes Before Breakthrough

If you're in a shaking situation, you are just on the other side of a great calm. The key to breaking through is to break out and go for it. You have to say, "I don't care what history says. I don't care what people say. I know God has given me a promise."

You need to realize that times of shaking will happen in your life. In fact, the worse the shaking times, the more glorious the breakthroughs. But you can't start with the breakthrough. You need to start by breaking out in your own mind and in your own faith.

If you're in a shaking situation, you are just on the other side of a great calm.

What does that mean, "break out"? Break out of what? Break out of self-imposed limitations. Break out of negative thinking. Break out of insecurities. Break out of fears. Break out of past failures. Break out of where you came from and the limitations that were put on you. Break out of depression and hopelessness. Break out of a self-defeating mentality that says, "Nothing's ever going to change in my life." If you break out, then God's breakthrough can happen.

When God's breakthrough happens, it means that Satan's line of defense has been shattered, so the breakthrough has to do with the enemy. But the breakout also has to do with you.

Instead of saying, "I need a breakthrough," you need to start saying, "I need a breakout."

> Instead of saying, "I need a breakthrough," you need to start saying, "I need a breakout."

The fulfillment of your dreams will not happen overnight. But you don't have to wait forever for a breakthrough. You can stir yourself to break out of whatever mind-set is holding you back.

One Against Six Hundred

The Philistines were the terrorists of the world about three thousand years ago. They were a murderous, aggressive people, and they roamed around killing anybody who got in their way.

There's a story in the Book of Judges about how a farmer named Shamgar saved Israel from destruction by single-handedly killing six hundred Philistines with an ox goad.

One of the best things to
learn from a seeming failure is to
pick yourself up and try again.
You break out of what didn't work,
and you say to yourself,
"Well, now I know what doesn't work.
Now I can mark that off the list."

The Book of Judges mentions Shamgar's name twice: "After him came Shamgar the son of Anath, who struck down six hundred Philistines with an ox goad; and he also saved Israel" (Judges 3:31, nas). "In the days of Shamgar the son of Anath, in the days of Jael, the highways were unoccupied, and the travellers walked through byways" (Judges 5:6).

Killing six hundred strong men by yourself seems like an impossible feat, and yet Shamgar succeeded. I see three keys to his success. Some of us face incredible odds. Our odds may not be six hundred to one, but they're bad enough.

Shamgar succeeded when a lesser man would have failed, all because he stepped out on three simple truths:

1. He started where he was.
2. He used what he had.
3. He did what he could.

He started where he was. He was a farmer, and he started in his field. The field where he grew his crops became his battlefield.

He was just a farmer who had a family and neighbors and no protection at all from the Philistines. He realized that if anything was going to change concerning his future, he would have to do something about it personally.

In the New Testament, we read "Be instant [prepared] in season, out of season" (2 Tim. 4:2). We're supposed to be prepared and ready for whatever happens. The word *season* in Greek has to do with opportunity. In other words, we had better be preparing ourselves now when it looks like nothing is happening, because the season will change and the opportunity to act will appear. When an opportunity comes, you need to be prepared for it

Shamgar *used what he had*. His resources were extremely limited. All he had was his ox goad. What's your "ox goad"? God has given you one. He has provided something that you can use in the situation you're in. He wants to show you what it is, and He wants you to use it with confidence and strength, taking what you have and applying every ounce of your ability to use it well.

Give God what you have,
and the miracle can happen.

Shamgar used what he had, which was his ox goad—and his enthusiasm. Did you know that our word *enthusiasm* comes from a Greek root, *entheos*, which means "in God," or even "possessed by a god." If you're in God and God is in you, you should be brimming with enthusiasm.

Give God what you have, and the miracle can happen. The miracle comes from what you already have, not from what you don't have. Let's *do what we can* with the resources we already have. We have an extra secret weapon that Shamgar doesn't mention, and that's prayer. With prayer in our arsenal, we can do a lot more than we can without it.

It is impossible to overexaggerate the importance of prayer to the success of everything you do. When Jesus said, "Whatever you ask in My name, I'll do it," He was talking about prayer. (See John 14:13.) All things are possible if you pray.

A Word About Faith Versus Fear

Fear comes in two categories:

1. Fear that I won't get what I need
2. Fear that I won't be able to hold on to what I have

Anybody who ever beat the odds or made a difference did it in spite of their fear. What are you waiting for—a feeling of courage? Forget it! It doesn't exist. You're only courageous when you do what's right despite your fears!

See if you can figure out what you're afraid of. If you can name it, you can conquer it. And understand this: fear attracts Satan like faith attracts God.

The Bible is a David-and-Goliath book. It teaches you that with God on your side, you're bigger than any problem. The question is, do you believe that enough to step out and allow God to use you? If you're just believing God for things you can do for yourself, you're limiting Him. Furthermore, if you think He'll never ask you to do things you can't do, think again! Jesus told one man to walk on water and another to come out of his grave—and they did!

When you find yourself experiencing things that are beyond your ability, that's when you know God is at work.

Everything big starts with
something small. All God needs
is something to start with!

Miracles only begin when you take what you have and put it into his hands. The moment you make it available to Him, it will begin to grow. Get rid of your life-limiting thoughts! Start dreaming! When God defines you, what difference does anybody else's opinion make?

Instead of comparing yourself to others, recognize what God has called you to be, accept the gifts He's given you, and start building on them. Everything big starts with something small. All God needs is something to start with!

Living in the Faith Zone

Whatever season you are in, God wants you to learn to say, "I cannot do this in my own strength. I need to lean on Him." You'll never have all the answers, so you might as well leave the risk-free "safe zone," where you can figure out the next step and where you can handle whatever comes your way, in favor of living in the faith zone.

As I said earlier, living in the faith zone means reaching up and grabbing hold of nothing and holding on to it until it becomes something. God wants you to live there. In fact, He wants you to live there so much that He will stretch you again and again.

Let Him Challenge You

Let God challenge you to step out on nothing. When you move out into the faith zone, you'll find out that that's where God lives.

If you're in God's perfect will, you may find yourself feeling very unsafe at times. You will feel extremely uncomfortable. But you will learn to depend on the Lord as you never could learn back in the comfort of your safe zone. Remember, when a God-given opportunity comes along, it's God's gift to you. What you do with that opportunity is your gift to God.

When a God-given opportunity
comes along, it is God's gift to you.
What you do with that opportunity
is your gift to God.

If you're in the safe zone, you don't really have to pray and seek God for anything because you feel OK about what you have already. You don't really have to be anointed because you can do everything without the anointing. Even though the security of the safe zone is what we try to achieve our whole life long, it's not God's will for His children. His will is that His children will always be dependent upon Him. Always.

If you want to be where God is, break out of the risk-free safe zone and start living in the faith zone. It's risky, but the faith zone is where God lives!

As long as you stay in the safe zone, you're not going to grow. You can't stay the same and learn at the same time. Many are so afraid to risk anything that they just stay behind closed doors. It's like they live their entire lives in Egypt, in the land of "not enough." Some people break out and take one step of faith—and they wind up in the wilderness, the land of "just enough." If they continue in a forward direction, living by faith, the day will come when they will enter their promised land.

> As long as you stay in the safe zone,
> you're not going to grow.

Open yourself up to the Holy Spirit, and tell Him, "Lord, I want to give You my fears. I turn my whole life over to You. I want to live in faith. I believe; help my unbelief! Fill me with courage, and furnish me with faith. I need it. I want to walk in Your will."

Feeding Your Faith

It's all part of the process of dream fulfillment. Every stage of the fulfillment of your dream depends on God. Even the so-called obstacles become important stepping-stones instead of barriers. Let's take a closer look at what I'm talking about. What are some things that you might consider to be obstacles that, in God's view, are merely stages in the process? Here are six that I can think of:

1. Your God-ordained purpose may be threatened, even from its birth.
2. Your God-ordained dream may be contaminated by godless influences.
3. You may experience serious failures.
4. You may be rejected.
5. You may feel personally inadequate.
6. Your God-ordained dream may require an unusually lengthy preparation time.

You can see how any of these could feed discouragement and defeat instead of success. But can you see how they could also feed your faith?

If you get rejected, what's the only way to make that negative event into something positive? The only way is to turn—in faith—to the One who never will reject you. When you do that, you turn the sizable obstacle of rejection into something that is more like a sizable step up toward God. It becomes a sizable step toward the fulfillment of His will for your life.

You can do it.

[Look] unto Jesus, the author and finisher of our faith, who for the joy that was set before Him endured the cross, despising the shame, and has sat down at the right hand of the throne of God.

—*Hebrews 12:2, nkjv*

Taking Hold:

- Shamgar killed six hundred Philistines with his ox goad. He started where he was, used what he had, and did what he could.
- In the process of walking toward the fulfillment of your dream, you can expect even the so-called obstacles to become important stepping-stones to faith.
- God wants you to live in the "faith zone," and that entails stepping out of your obstacle-free "safe zone."

Chapter 8

Don't Let Go of Your Dream

*R*eaching your dream requires a process—it takes time, persistence, patience. In this chapter we will discover the importance of holding tightly to your dream and discover how to enjoy the process, even if it takes a long time and leads you through an uncharted course that requires your total faith and commitment.

Ecclesiastes 9:10 says, "Whatever your hand finds to do, do it with your might" (nkjv). That means to give yourself diligently to the task at hand. It involves passion, determination and excellence. It's the opposite of just getting by or doing the minimum requirement.

The secret to discovering your destiny is to find something you enjoy doing so much that you would be willing to do it for free. Then, become so good at it that people are willing to pay you to do it.

...And Then Some

I want to give you three words that can transform your life: and then some.

I want to introduce you to an "and then some" person in Genesis 24. When it was time for Isaac to be married, his father, Abraham, sent his trusted servant Eleazar to find a wife. Eleazar put out a fleece before God, essentially saying, "God, may the right woman you want to marry Isaac offer water for me to drink and my camels also."

He went to the well of water and waited. Suddenly a beautiful woman walks up to Eleazar and offers him some water. And then she says, "Sir, by the way, I will inconvenience myself for a minimum of three to four hours, and I will water your camels also."

In the Old Testament, it was customary to offer water to a stranger. It was part of the Hebrew culture that you treat strangers kindly. So, here's the point. When Rebekah walked up to him and said, "Would you like some water?" that was what was required of her. That was normal. But when she added these words, "And I'll water your camels also," everything changed, because what she was saying was, "I'm going to do what is expected of me and then some."

One of the greatest life lessons that you can ever grab hold of is this: don't just do what's expected. Do what's expected and then some.

Don't just do what your job description says,
what people expect you to do.
Do what's expected and then some.

The philosophy of most people is: "How little can I do and get by with it? I'm just going to do what's expected of me. I'm just going to do what other people do, and that's enough." But, no, it's not good enough! If you are a Christian, you're supposed to do what you're expected to do—and then some.

The difference between a highly successful person and an average person is those three words: and then some.

I believe possibly one of the greatest tools for evangelism in this culture is not a pulpit. It could be in the workplace where people don't just do a get-by job. Christians shouldn't go into a job tomorrow morning with the mentality, "I'll do my quota; I'll only do what's expected." They should go to that workplace every day as a lifestyle, thinking in their mind, "I'm going to do what's expected and go a little bit beyond." If Christians started operating in this principle, do you know what the first question on every job application would be? It would be, "Are you a Christian?"

They see how you work, and that
gives you a platform into their life.

Jesus said, "Let your light so shine before men, that they may see your good works, and glorify your Father which is in heaven" (Matt. 5:16). They see how you work, and that gives you a platform into their life.

When Rebekah went out there and watered those camels, she had no idea what the ramifications would be. She was doing this as a lifestyle. She was a kind person, and she was used to doing what was expected—and then some. She just kept doing what was right in God's eyes.

From this story I see five things you must do to release God's will in your life:

1. Don't Despise Small Things
Faithfulness with small things brings huge rewards. God is your boss. He's watching you when you're faithful in the small things. Big doors swing on little hinges.

2. Don't Wait for the Big Moments

Big moments don't come to people who wait for big moments. Big moments come out of faithfulness in little, insignificant moments of doing routine, menial things that are non-glamorous and not really exciting. The big moment comes out of being faithful with the little things.

3. Help People

Rebekah didn't quote a scripture. She just said, "I'm going to help you." Now, isn't that a witness? Isn't that a different approach? Instead of trying to be superspiritual, why don't we just be a nice person and help somebody? She gave a stranger some water and then took care of his camels.

4. Do Your Best—and Then Some

You can't go the second mile until you do the first mile. Can people trust you when they turn their back and walk away and never wonder if you're going to do the job right? If you help somebody with their dream, God will reveal yours to you.

5. When God Opens the Door, Walk Through It

Eleazar saw Rebekah, at her own expense and time, serve water to those camels. Afterward, he said, "Let me tell you who I am, and let me tell you who you are. It just came out of your work ethic. You're the chosen bride-to-be. Come with me."

We keep waiting on supernatural promotion. We say, "Anoint me for promotion." But if you don't do your side on the natural, God can't open the door for the supernatural, because you wouldn't have the integrity and character and work ethic if He does give you that promotion.

> When you give extra effort, it always opens doors.
> And when God opens the door, don't be intimidated.

The Bible says that her brother and mother said, "We're excited. We're thrilled about this, but we need ten days." The servant said, "We're not waiting ten days. You come now, or you miss it." Notice that when you give extra effort, it always opens doors. And when God opens the door, don't back up. Don't be intimidated. Don't be embarrassed. Don't say, "I'm not good enough." Don't say, "Well, somebody else could do it better." If God wanted somebody else to do it, He would have put them where you are.

If an opportunity comes your way and God opens a door, stand up, step up and walk through that door, because God will go with you. God will make up for what you don't have. He will make up for the abilities that you don't have.

"Give Me This Mountain"

Caleb was one of the twelve spies whom Moses sent out into the Promised Land, which was occupied by other people groups at the time. While he was on that spying mission, Caleb spotted a particular mountain. He wanted it for his own. This gave Caleb a definite purpose in life, a purpose that was big enough and exciting enough to keep him alive for a long time. He eventually did reach his dream of owning that mountain. But he didn't get to have it quite so fast. In fact, forty long years had to pass before he could even bring it up again. By then, he was eighty-five years old, but God had preserved him. Finally, he could say, "Now therefore, give me this mountain of which the Lord spoke in that day" (Josh. 14:12, nkjv).

Let's look at the story in a little more detail because we can face some of the same hindrances that Caleb did, and we can learn from his experiences.

Fear of Giants

Ten of the spies had come back with alarm written all over their faces, saying, "There are giants in the land! We are not able!" The people picked up on their fear. Because of it, the people talked themselves out of a great miracle.

Only Caleb and Joshua had no fear. They had said, "God wants us to have this land. We are well able to take this land. God will be with us. Let's do it!"

There's never any provision without a problem first.

The people just wouldn't buy it. They were like so many of us. Even when we see the evidence of what God is leading us to do, we don't go after it, because we're waiting for the coast to clear. We're waiting until we can take a shot at getting some of the grapes without having to face any giants. There's never any provision without a problem first. If you're going to hold back and wait until it looks like a problem-free journey ahead, you'll never get the grapes.

When David went out to fight the giant Goliath, he did not back down. To get ahead, you too are going to have to first face a giant. You are going to have to do it yourself. You cannot send somebody else to do it for you. If you avoid giants because you are afraid, and if you want a giant-free, conflict-free, problem-avoiding life, you will never get ahead at all.

Grasshoppers

Here's what the fearful spies had said:

> And there we saw the giants, the sons of Anak, which come of the giants: and we were in our own sight as grasshoppers, and so we were in their sight.
>
> —*Numbers 13:33*

That means they perceived themselves as being as little and puny as grasshoppers compared to the inhabitants of Canaan. They thought the giants would be able to just step on them and crush them.

Grasshoppers can't run or fight. Grasshoppers have wings, but they can't fly. They can only get so high, and then they come back down.

We have wings too, and we're supposed to be able to soar

like eagles. Instead, we hop around like grasshoppers.

We don't have to stay that way, though. We can change our self-perception. We can start to soar like eagles if we want to. Our self-perception is so important. How we perceive ourselves is major, because other people will pick up on how we perceive ourselves.

Milk and Honey?

When the going gets a little tough, sometimes we start to think, as those Israelites did, that we should just go back to where we came from. We forget how bad it was back there. The Israelites said to Moses, "Is it not enough that you have brought us up out of a land flowing with milk and honey to have us die in the wilderness, but you would also lord it over us?" (Num. 16:13, nas).

Back in Egypt, they were slaves. Egypt was nowhere near a land of milk and honey for them. But in order to hold them back from reaching what God had in store for them, the enemy had to make them think that where they came from was better.

The enemy had to make them think
that where they came from was better.

Right now, some of us have come out of Egypt by the blood of Jesus. But we find ourselves in the middle of a wilderness. It's hard. We are struggling. We have lost our determination because of all the battles we have been through. All of a sudden, we think, "Hey, wait a minute! I didn't have these problems before I was saved," and that's probably true. Suddenly we want to go back.

Let me remind you: what you left behind was death, destruction and bondage. You don't want to go back to that.

Antidote to Fear

Below are three fears that you and I face on our journey to the land of dreams.

1. *Fear of faces.* The fear of faces is the fear of people. It's the fear of what people will say, what people will think. No one can make you feel inferior without your consent. God told them not to be afraid of their faces.
2. *Fear of fences.* This is the fear of barriers and roadblocks. We're afraid that it will be too hard. It might hurt. Charles Lindbergh said, "Success is not measured by what a man accomplishes, but by the opposition he encountered and the courage he maintained in his struggle against it."
3. *Fear of failure.* Isn't that what really stops us every time? We like the idea of success. We like to win. It's the "what ifs" that get us. "What if I make a fool of myself? What if...what if..." And the next thing you know, you're back in your easy chair, not going anywhere.

Don't Get Talked Out of Your Vision

Moses had presented the vision clearly to the people of Israel. They could stop being slaves, and they wouldn't have to go back to Egypt. God was promising them a land for themselves. All they had to do was obey Him. He would help them.

Why was it so hard to do that? What stopped them?

This happens in churches all the time, and it can happen in businesses too. There's a clear goal. You're on your way to it. The promise is that you'll get there. Nobody is holding you back.

. . . except for that person, or usually more than one person, who is sitting right next to you. Or maybe it's you.

Why should the enemy exert himself to muster outside forces to come against you when he will have such an easy time stirring up internal objections? The twelve spies were chosen from the twelve tribes of Israel. They ended up being bigger enemies to the plan of God than the giants were. They talked Moses and the other leaders out of trying to acquire the land of promise.

What did God do? He took care of the problem by letting them stay "safe." "Safe" meant they'd have to keep wandering in the wilderness for forty more years while that whole generation died and a new generation could replace them.

God's plan could still succeed, only with different players. God would keep their vision alive, but He wouldn't let them fulfill it after all. He would let their sons and daughters fulfill it instead.

Taking Hold:

- The secret to discovering your destiny is to find something you enjoy doing so much that you would be willing to do it for free.
- Don't just do what your job description says. Do what's expected and then some.
- If an opportunity comes your way and God opens a door, stand up, step up, and walk through that door, because God will go with you.
- Don't get talked out of your vision.

Chapter 9

Keep Climbing

*O*ur limitations are mostly in our minds, often in our spirits, and sometimes in our bodies. To fulfill the vision God gives us for our lives, we have to break through old ways of thinking and acting. How we turn out spiritually and physically has so much to do with our minds.

Mountains Are for Climbing

In the Swiss Alps, there is a little mountain day camp for rookie climbers. Many businesses go there and take their employees for an outing. They'll start out early in the morning and load on their climbing gear, and then they'll climb halfway up a mountain. When they get halfway up, there's something they call "the halfway house." They get there around noon. They take off their gear, go in for a warm meal and sit in front of the beautiful fireplace. The trip sponsors say that every time, without exception, when it's time for lunch to be over and time to strap their gear back on, they lose half the people. Half of them are content to stay and never complete the journey. They're content to go only halfway up.

So, they stay in the halfway house and lounge around and play games and sing by the piano. They sit by the fire and enjoy themselves. Then around four o'clock in the afternoon, they all hear a bell outside. They walk over and look out the big window that faces the mountain. That's when they see their friends summiting that mountain! The halfway house hosts say the party atmosphere turns instantly into a funeral atmosphere, because now the people who chose to stay behind realize that their friends, who were willing to keep going, have just had the experience of a lifetime, while they stayed behind, complacent and settled. Now they wish they could be celebrating on the mountaintop too, but it's too late.

Many times, it would
seem to be easier just to settle.

114

This is a vivid picture of how our lives can be, isn't it? Many times, it would seem to be easier just to settle. But, of course, it's obvious that you will never reach your mountaintop if you quit.

Quitters

We all know some quitters. Quitters just don't try anymore. They tend to be "victims" of something or somebody, and they can become bitter and depressed. It's kind of a drag to be around them. Quitters wish things would be easier. They don't have a lot of endurance. When things get the least bit difficult, quitters quit.

There are two times when you'll
be the most vulnerable to quitting:
when you've suffered a great failure and
when you've just had a great success.

Just to forewarn you, there are two times when you'll be the most vulnerable to quitting. The first is when you've suffered a great failure. The second, believe it or not, is when you've just had a great success. The first one isn't a surprise. And the second one isn't either, if you think about it, because after you succeed, you can soon become complacent.

The life of Jesus included a lot of suffering. That never

stopped Him. Look what He did, especially when He went ahead and climbed Calvary. He was definitely not a quitter.

> [Look] unto Jesus the author and finisher of our faith; who for the joy that was set before him endured the cross, despising the shame, and is set down at the right hand of the throne of God.
>
> —*Hebrews 12:2*

Campers

Then we come to the campers, the ones who climb for a while and then decide they like it well enough halfway up the mountain. They decide to camp out and enjoy the view. They achieve some aspect of their goal, and then they're satisfied. They grow weary of the never-ending climb.

Campers join the halfway club. They're not total quitters, but they're not going to make it to the top any more than the quitters are. As a group, they've lost their edge. They begin to see the campground as their permanent address. They have achieved partial success, and that seems to be enough for them.

Climbers

God wants you to be a climber. Just as He showed Caleb his mountain and kept him working toward it, He gives you a dream, and He wants to help you reach it.

To be a climber, you have to be dedicated. You have to put up with discomfort and fatigue. Climbers adopt the mentality that camping places are like base camps. In their view, what they have achieved up to that point is the launching pad for the future, not their final address.

The mountain you are climbing may look insurmountable. Now that you're climbing it, you may not be able to see the top of it anymore. But if you are a climber, you just keep putting one foot in front of the other. You take provisions and refreshment where you can get them, while keeping your ultimate goal in the front of your mind. "I am climbing this mountain because I'm going to conquer it. I am going to reach the top."

Climbers are the people who
see obstacles as opportunities.

Climbers are the people who see obstacles as opportunities. They're the people who, regardless of misfortune and disadvantage, pain or past achievements, keep on climbing until they reach the top.

Eventually, you will make it. But did you know that the most dangerous time for a climber isn't while the climber is still going up? The most dangerous time is coming back down. That says to me that you need to keep your climbing mentality even after you've achieved your desire.

If you're a climber, you will hear things from God whether you're headed up or whether you're headed back down. He will be climbing with you.

You are not old until your regrets take the place of your dream. Regret looks back. Worry looks around. Vision looks up. Vision sees the mountaintop even when the clouds hide it from view. Enduring the climb now equals enjoyment later. Breaking through limitations and barriers now equals victory later.

God will help you climb. He will climb with you, and He will lend you a hand every day. He will help you break through limitation thinking, and He will help you climb your mountain.

Taking Hold:

- God does not have any limits. But we do—or we think we do. He will help us break through limitation thinking. All things are possible with Him!
- You need to press forward, keeping your dream alive, not only breaking through fears, misconceptions, lies from the enemy, and bad advice, but also learning to ignore the voice that tells you to take it easy.
- God wants you to be a climber, not a quitter or a camper.
- Regret looks back. Worry looks around. Vision looks up. Vision sees the mountaintop even when the clouds hide it from view. Breaking through limitations and barriers now equals victory later.

Chapter 10

Never Doubt Your Vision

What do you do when your world does not look like your word; when you have a word from God over your life, but your present situation doesn't look like the dream God gave you?

God told Abraham, "You have security. You have success. You have servants. You have wealth. You have everything. But I want you to walk away from it." Hebrews 11:8 puts it like this: "By faith Abraham, when called to go to a place he would later receive as his inheritance, obeyed and went, even though he did not know where he was going" (niv). He knew where he was, but he didn't know where he was going.

In Genesis 22, the opposite was true for Abraham. Now he knows where he's going, but he doesn't know where he is. The man of faith is confused! He doesn't understand a thing that God is doing. What's going through his mind is, "God, where are You? I'm lost. I'm confused. All I know is that I heard a voice, and the voice said, 'Go.' But I don't know where I am right now. I know You made me a promise, but where I am doesn't look like anything You showed me in my spirit." He was three days from "a place." It's a place I'm going to call "three days from nowhere."

"After These Things…"

Genesis 22 starts out by saying, "After these things…" I believe Abraham thought the worst trials of his faith were in his past. I believe he thought he had finally arrived, because now he had Isaac, his promised seed. He had the promise.

Sometimes you think your big trials are in your past. If God's going to introduce greater revelations of who He is and greater dimensions of His power, it will be "after these things."

Just when you think you've been through it all, seen it all, and fought every demon that hell could bring, here comes the big one—the trial of a lifetime!

"After these things," God said to Abraham, "leave where you are and go a three days' journey, and I'll tell you what to do."

He takes his boy, Isaac, to that mountain. God's biggest point to Abraham was this: "Though you're one hundred and twenty years old, don't relax! I know you think your big trials are in the past, but I'm not through with you. And the way that you know I'm not through with you is that I'm going to do something mighty in your future. You'll know it because I have to send you through a season of trials, of feeling like you're confused and lost…a time when you will be "three days from nowhere.'"

Three Days From Nowhere

"Abraham, you may not know where I am, and you may not know what's going on. That's a sign that I'm about to trust you with your greatest blessing yet! So take Isaac, 'laughter,' put him on an altar, and kill him!"

Sometimes when you're "three days from nowhere," you are in a mind battle. You're confused. You don't know where God is. You don't know where you are. You know where you're going, but this doesn't look like where you're supposed to be at this time in your life. At this phase, you thought you would be further along. Instead, you're "three days from nowhere"!

Everybody has his or her trial of a lifetime. The other trials are just faith boosters to get your immune system up. Then comes the big one, the trial of a lifetime.

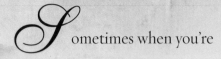

$\mathcal{S}$ometimes when you're

"three days from nowhere,"

you are in a mind battle.

But it's the trial of a

lifetime that leads to the

experience of a lifetime.

> It's the trial of a lifetime that leads
> to the experience of a lifetime.

But it's the trial of a lifetime that leads to the experience of a lifetime. The Bible says three times that Abraham lifted up his eyes. In Genesis 18:2 he lifted up his eyes and saw three men at his tent door. One of them was God, and Abraham fed Him a meal. At that point, God started giving promises. He said, "As the sand...upon the sea shore," so shall your seed be (Gen. 22:17).

So, the first level, when he lifted up his eyes, is the receiving of the promise.

But then the Scripture says again in Genesis 22:4, "Abraham lifted up his eyes, and saw the place afar off." Now it's gone beyond just receiving the promise. You actually begin to step into the destiny that God has for you. There's one other level that you get to, though, and that's in Genesis 22:13: "Abraham lifted up his eyes...and behold behind him a ram..."

> The truth is, God has to bring all men
> and women whom He has a destiny for to a
> place called "three days from nowhere."

You only get that level of blessing when you go through "three days from nowhere." When you go through such a severe trial

125

of a lifetime, it feels like everything is gone, you have missed God, and you feel like you've blown it and messed up.

The truth is, God has to bring all men and women whom He has a destiny for to a place that is called "three days from nowhere."

The Scripture says that God proved and showed Himself to be Jehovah-Jireh at that place (Gen. 22:14). Abraham did not call Him Jehovah-Jireh when he got to the mountain and saw the provision. He called Him Jehovah-Jireh down at the foot of the mountain when his boy asked him, "Father, where's the lamb?" Abraham said, "God will provide himself a lamb" (Gen. 22:7–8).

Anybody can call Him Jehovah-Jireh when you get on top of the problem. But don't wait until you get on the mountain to call Him Jehovah-Jireh. Abraham called Him Jehovah-Jireh when he was still three days from nowhere!

If you're three days from nowhere, God's letting you know that He's with you. You may not know where you're going, but you know who's going with you. And if He's with you, it doesn't matter what you're going through!

Don't wait until you get
on the mountain to call
Him Jehovah-Jireh.

It's only a matter of time before you're faced with such a severe trial that you find yourself "three days from nowhere." You have no answers, you're confused, you're stunned, and you feel a little hurt by God.

But if you have to understand everything before you will trust and serve God, you don't understand the concept of faith!

If you get in a storm in the
will of God, lift up your eyes.

Can you see Abraham as he raised the knife? God said, "Stop, Abraham. Now I know. I had to put you through the trial of a lifetime to reveal to you the greatest revelation of who 'the Lamb' is."

Every true dream God gives will make the same trek as Abraham's dream made through the place of confusion. You'll wake up one day and find yourself three days from nowhere. But remember, on Friday they crucified our Lord. Three days later, He rose again. You may feel confused, broken, and discouraged. You're just three days from nowhere. It's Friday, but Sunday's coming!

Even though your promise may be postdated,
remember whose signature is on the check!

Your appointment is still on God's calendar. "There has never been the slightest doubt in my mind that the God who started the great work in you would keep at it and bring it to a flourishing finish" (Phil. 1:6, *The Message*).

God works on both ends of the timeline. He gets you ready for "it" (even when you don't know what "it" is) and He gets "it" ready for you. Even though your promise may be post-dated, remember whose signature is on the check! To get from where you are to where you're going, you have to be willing to be in-between. Have you been asking the Lord how long your passion and dream will be "there" while your place is "here"? Remember: just before He opens new doors and new opportunities that give birth to new dreams, you'll go through a place called "three days from nowhere." When you do, never doubt your vision.

Never Doubt Your Vision

I know that God will back up the dreams and visions that He puts into people's hearts. You should never doubt your vision because you should never doubt your God.

It doesn't matter how long it takes to see your dream come to fruition. It doesn't matter if your vision is a big one or a little one. If God is in it, it's in the bag. If He inspired it in the first place, He will see it through to completion.

As I was praying, I heard people crying, "How long, O Lord?" I've just come to tell you that you're not out of the will of God. You're three days from nowhere. This is the trial of a lifetime, and if you'll hold on, it's going to become the blessing of a lifetime. You will see the Lamb in all of His glory.

So What If They Don't Believe?

So what if "they" say it won't happen? So what if people laugh and mock the dream that God has given you? The simple fact is this: Your God is a rock. He will not fail.

Other people don't have to believe in you in order for your dream to come true. It's your dream. God gave it to you, not to them. You're the dream carrier, and what God plans to do does not depend upon the affirmation of the people around you.

When all the voices around you tell you that you cannot accomplish the dream that God has given you and that it will not happen, God wants you to be able to say, "So what if they don't believe? They can't cancel out what God has put into me."

When you have a real dream, "they" can throw you into a pit and your dream will still happen! Remember Joseph? When you have a real dream, "they" can lie about you and defame your good name. Even if "they" overlook you for promotion and ignore you and act as if they never heard of you, God will see your dream through. So what if they don't believe?

If you have a real dream from God, it won't die in the face of opposition.

How Can You Be Sure?

Everything I said above applies to you only if your dream matches God's plan for your life. How can you be sure it does?

If it's not God's dream, He's not obligated to back it up. You need to identify the origin of your dream. Not all dreams are God's dreams.

Many times, people say they have a dream, but it's really somebody else's dream. Sometimes parents are bad in this regard. They want to relive some part of their life through you, so they assign something to you that they always wanted to do. They didn't get to do it, so they want their child to do it. That sets you up for a lifetime of trying to please your mother or father. Finally one day, you wake up and realize that you are trying to live up to somebody else's dream. You're trying to fulfill somebody else's expectations.

You need to identify the origin of your dream. It doesn't matter how many years you have spent trying to chase that dream—if it's not your dream from God, don't bother with it. Don't let anyone cram a dream into your heart that just doesn't fit.

Don't let anyone cram a dream into
your heart that just doesn't fit.

Another kind of dream that you should stop carrying is the kind that's tainted by pride or jealousy or anger or rejection. Are you trying to prove something to somebody? Don't go there. Are you trying to make up for being rejected? Ask the Lord to help you get past it. Ask Him to give you a real dream straight from heaven, a dream that He can back up.

Take Inventory

You have to take inventory of the gifts and talents and resources that God has given you and see if they match up with the dream you think is from God.

Do it honestly. Don't say you have talents you wish you had. Don't lie to yourself.

Your resources, gifts and talents should provide an indication of what God's dream is for your life. They should also let you know some things that you're not gifted to do so that you don't go out and try to do them (and fail).

I believe that when God gives you a dream, He supplies you with everything you need to fulfill that dream.

You won't have to beg, borrow, or steal someone else's resources in order to fulfill your dream from God. You can just relax and trust God to collect your own resources at the right time and in the right way.

You don't have to wish you were somebody else. Don't try to masquerade as somebody else. God says, "I'm not going to use somebody else for this one. You're going to push this one out!" He made you for a purpose, and He wants you to walk in the glory of it.

Taking Hold:

- Never doubt your vision. If God gave it to you, even if it seems far away, you can count on His help to achieve it.
- Let God adjust your vision if He needs to. He usually needs to make some changes inside you before you're ready to pursue your dream.
- Be on the lookout for your next mountain. God wants to give you another vision that will build on this one.
- Don't be discouraged if other people don't agree with your vision. They don't have to for it to be valid. Decide if your dream is really from God, and then go for it with your whole heart.

Chapter 11

Never Too Old

*J*ust when you think you can retire, don't be surprised if God puts a new mantle on you. You see, God has a plan for your life in the now.

Whether you're old or not, married or not, settled and secure or not, you need to know that your God has a purpose and a mission for you right now. How can I be so sure that He does, when I don't even know you? Because you're still here. As long as you have a purpose, you'll keep on living. You're never too old for God.

Father Abraham

If anybody could have retired comfortably, it would have been Abraham. He was a wealthy man. He was seventy-five years old. But then God came knocking. Genesis 12 tells how God told him to pack up and leave his land and his countrymen behind and to launch on a journey to somewhere. God didn't say where. He did promise to make a great nation of his offspring. But wait a minute—Abraham and Sarah had never had any children, and now they were too old.

I'm sure his wife wondered if he was in his right mind. Abraham just said, "I realize I don't know where we're going. We have to go because we have to obey God."

Abraham had no concept of the importance of his decision. What was God's mission for Abraham? It was no less than to populate the entire Middle East! The mission and purpose that he said yes to involved the establishment of the Jews, God's own people, in their own land. Abraham would become the father of so many generations that nobody would be able to count them.

What Made Him Do It?

Why would an old guy like Abraham pack up and leave for the wilderness? I see five dynamics at work, and you can learn a few things from them—even if you're not anywhere near the age of seventy-five yet.

Abraham had the following in his life:

1. The ability to hear God
2. The ability to believe what God said
3. The ability to denounce security for the sake of God's mission
4. The ability to stay focused on the mission
5. The ability to accomplish the mission

He Had the Ability to Hear God

We read, "The Lord had said unto Abram..." How did the Lord say it? Was it an audible voice? Maybe. All we know is that Abram had the ability to hear what God said. That implies that he had some kind of a relationship with the Lord. He recognized the voice of the Lord because he had heard it before.

How does that apply to you and me? How do we hear the voice? Even with our Bibles and other people around us who can help us hear God, the same basic, underlying relationship with God is a prerequisite. You will never really hear God until you have developed a relationship with Him. Then you'll recognize His voice. When God speaks, you just know it's Him.

If you say, "Well, that's never happened to me," then you should be asking for a closer relationship with Him. Christianity is not religion. It's about relationship.

You will never really hear God until you have developed a relationship with Him.

If you will spend time in the Word and start reading it every day, and if you start praying and talking to Him, your ability to hear God will increase dramatically. It's the same with the people you love. The more you spend time with them, the better you understand them. Spend time with God. Become His friend, and you will recognize His voice when He speaks to you.

God doesn't save you and show you His power just to get you to heaven. He wants you to keep following Him right here on Earth. God came and showed you a quick glimpse of your future purpose and mission, and then He took off. He wants you to apprehend that for which you were apprehended. You have to develop big Mickey Mouse ears in your spirit so that you can hear Him, even when what He says doesn't make a lot of sense to people.

When God says something, it will make enough sense to you. It made enough sense to Abraham. Abraham picked up and moved. Swallowing their objections, everybody else went with him.

He Had the Ability to Believe What God Said

It's one thing to hear God. You also have to believe what you hear Him say. The Book of Hebrews talks about Abraham's ability to believe:

*I*t's a good idea to tell your mind to believe the next thing you hear from God. Tell yourself, "I'm going to start believing what I hear. I'm not going to back up. I'm not going to waver. I refuse to vacillate."

By faith Abraham obeyed when he was called to go out to the place which he would receive as an inheritance. And he went out, not knowing where he was going.

—*Hebrews 11:8, nkjv, emphasis mine*

The Book of Hebrews also tells us that without faith it's impossible to please God (Heb. 11:6). Abraham pleased God with his faith.

Abraham believed because he knew that God is always right. He knew that His mind does not run along the same tracks as our minds do.

It's a good idea to tell your mind to believe the next thing you hear from God. Don't hem and haw and wait for another "sign" or another word of prophecy. Just believe what you hear Him say.

He Had the Ability to Renounce Security for the Sake of God's Mission

Abraham was as comfortable and secure as a man could get in those days. And yet he had the ability to make a divine denunciation of his present blessing in favor of the future promise.

If you are going to move into the purpose of God in your life, a time will come when you too will have to remove yourself from the safe, predictable place. When that time comes, you'll have to believe that you really heard God and that He can be trusted to bring you into your promise.

You can have faith that God knows what He's doing because Abraham launched out in faith, and many others have done it too.

He Had the Ability to Stay Focused on the Mission

Abram could have just changed his mind. He could have had second thoughts, especially after his wife began to wonder aloud what was going to become of them if they left Ur and went out into the howling wilderness.

But Abram stuck to it, and he kept on packing. He didn't worry about his advanced age or all of the other reasons he could have used to justify staying put.

He didn't change his mind once they set out, either. Now, instead of having a settled lifestyle, they were nomadic. But Abraham had set his face to obey God, so he didn't let the challenges of his new lifestyle shake his decision.

Different kinds of problems came up all the time. Abraham could have decided it just wasn't worth it. Why on earth had God sent him on this wild goose chase anyway? He hadn't told him why. God had just said GO!

He Had the Ability to Accomplish the Mission

Because he had the ability to hear God and believe Him, and because he had the ability to renounce his security and stay focused on his mission, Abraham had the most important ability of all—he had the ability to accomplish the mission.

He had never done anything like this before. It took years. Abraham had to hear God, believe God and obey God quite a few times in order to accomplish the mission of positioning himself for the future. He didn't wait until all his questions were answered. He took things as they came, one at a time. He kept his focus, even though he didn't always do everything perfectly.

The most important ability of all is
the ability to accomplish the mission.

The main thing about Abraham was that he launched and he didn't turn back. I think God likes someone like that, someone who takes risks, even if they're foolish ones sometimes. If all the questions have to be answered before you step out and obey God, you'll never do anything.

Ready, Aim, Fire

You may remember how, when Elijah was about to be taken to heaven, Elisha asked for a double portion of his master's spirit, and he got it.

Elisha went on to do many exploits, and eventually he became an old man. This is where I want to pick up the story, because part of Elisha's "double-portion" mission was to speak into the life of the king of Israel about one of his missions, but the king's response wasn't bold enough to suit Elisha. (See 2 Kings 13:14–19, nkjv.)

Real victory is not won on the battlefield; it's won behind the scenes. Real victory is won in your private life, in your "bedchamber," if you will. Real victory is won in your inner man first, and then you will see evidence on the battlefield.

Our public success or
failure reflects what happens
in our private life.

So Elisha had King Joash with him in his bedchamber, and he said to King Joash, "Take a bow and arrows." He took them privately. It's like when we take up our weapons of prayer every morning in private. What we do with them is important. Our public success or failure reflects what happens in our private life. The two always coordinate with each other; the public manifests the private.

Elisha had the king pick up his weapon, even though he was just in Elisha's private room and not out on the battlefield, fighting against Syria. In the same way, God will have us pick up our weapons in our private prayer times. That's where the real business gets transacted. That's where you really pick

We need to start talking healing when we're feeling sick. We need to start talking blessing and prosperity when we don't have anything. We need to talk about living when we feel like dying. We need to speak about marching when we feel like quitting.

up your weapons, because there's no point in faking it anyway. It doesn't matter if you're not much of a warrior.

Joash was the old king, and he was losing on the battlefield. Elisha was an old man, and he was a prophet; he'd never been a warrior. But they could both obey the Word of the Lord if they wanted to.

We need to start talking victory
when we're staring at defeat.

The king picked up his bow and arrow, and he shot once out the window, as Elisha said. It's the same with us, except our "arrows" are our words. Our arrows are our confession, and our worship and our prayers. We need to let them fly out of us. We need to start talking victory when we're staring at defeat. That's how we shoot our word arrows.

Elisha didn't shoot the arrows for the king. He told him what to do, but the king had to do it himself.

After the king shot one arrow, Elisha told him to take the rest of the arrows and start striking the ground with them. King Joash did it. He hit the ground with the arrows hard three times.

But Elisha was furious. He said, "Why did you stop?" Because if he had kept hitting the ground even a couple more times, he would have been assured of complete victory over his enemies. But he stopped short of that. Now he would win some battles, but he wouldn't win the war.

Don't we do that ourselves sometimes? We stop just short of God's best. We think that three times is good enough. It doesn't seem like anything is happening, so we quit.

The Devil Has Your Number

Don't slack off. You need to keep doing what God told you to do. And you need to do it with some intensity! Sometimes when you are on the verge of a breakthrough, it's even more important to keep going. Too many people give up when they're right on the verge of a breakthrough. That can be the most discouraging time of all.

Instead of turning back, you need to say to yourself, "I'm too close to back up now." You need to recognize how the devil works against you. Discouragement is what he uses to make you quit, especially right before you're about to run through the finish line.

Next time you feel discouraged, don't quit. All it means is that the devil is so desperate to stop you that he has sent his most powerful weapon against you.

Don't Let Your Dream Die

Now, there's one more wonderful detail in this story of King Joash and Elisha. It's about Elisha himself, who had been faithfully pursuing his dream full steam ahead, all his life, and who had just taken time out to help the king.

The end of his life came soon after he helped Joash. He was sick already when he helped him. Soon, he died.

If you count the major miracles that his master Elijah had performed and then you count the number that Elisha did, you'll see that Elijah performed seven major miracles before he was taken up to heaven. Then Elisha put on his mantle, and he began to perform miracles. He had gotten up to thirteen when he died.

He was on his deathbed, one miracle short of two times seven, or a double portion. A double portion had been God's promise to him. Having a "double portion" of Elijah's miracle-working spirit was Elisha's God-given dream.

The same kind of thing can happen with you when you choose to give from your deficit. You encourage somebody even when you're discouraged yourself. When you reach out to somebody else, it's good for you. You get your focus off yourself, God takes pleasure in you, and your discouragement is dispelled. A sure way to get discouraged is to think about nothing but yourself.

So, it's as if Elisha died having given his last miracle to somebody else. People took Elisha's body, and they put it in a grave. Soon afterward, some people came to bury another dead man in the same cemetery. Just then, a Moabite raid rolled through. They had to get rid of the body in a hurry, so they put it in on top of Elisha's body in his sepulchre.

Then look what happened: Elisha didn't revive, but the other dead man did. (See 2 Kings 13:20–21.) When that dead body hit the bones of Elisha, it was miracle number fourteen!

The devil may have thought he managed to rob Elisha of the full double portion, but he didn't after all. God was faithful. Elisha's dream did not die with him. That's the kind of God we serve, every one of us.

What dream has God given you? What new dream has He added to the old ones? Whether you're just starting out or building on past dreams, what has God told you that He wants to do with you?

God is faithful. He will have you walking in the purpose of your dream if you say yes to Him. Say yes, and then do something to keep remembering where you're going. Above all, keep remembering how faithful God is. He keeps making your dream happen right up to, and past, the day of your physical death. Our faithful God is worthy of every word of praise we can ever proclaim!

Taking Hold:

- Because you're here, you can be sure that God has a plan and purpose for your life, whether you're old or young.
- Abraham packed up his wife and the whole company of his dependents and set out on a nomadic life. The only reason he would do this was because of these important characteristics. He had:
  - The ability to hear God
  - The ability to believe what God said
  - The ability to denounce security for the sake of God's mission
  - The ability to stay focused on the mission
  - The ability to accomplish the mission
- Abraham was a risk taker. So was Elisha. So was Peter. Are you a risk taker?
- God will always be faithful to His Word. God is so faithful, He will keep fulfilling His Word even after you die, which is what He did for Elisha and also for Jacob.

Chapter 12

Put Away Your Measuring Stick

*C*an you believe that you can? Can you believe the message of this book for your own life? Do you believe that you can reach your highest potential? Can you believe that all things are possible—for you—with your all-powerful God?

You can't create your own dream or choose your own dream, because it comes from God, and He is the One who needs to give it to you. But you can choose to let it live and thrive. You can decide to pick it up and run with it. You can purposely take hold of your destiny.

> You can't choose how you came into this world. But you can choose to be blessed.

You can't choose who your momma or your daddy are. You can't choose how you came into this world. But you can choose to be blessed. You can say yes to God's plan for your life. You were created for a purpose, and God wants you to walk in it.

When your Creator God made you and put you in your mother's womb, He took everything that you now consider negative about yourself, and He factored it in. He took everything that you now consider positive about yourself, and He factored that in too. He put it all into His computer, so to speak, and out came the wonderful plan God has for your life. He locked it up inside you, and He made two keys—one for you and one for Himself.

> You were created for a purpose, and God wants you to walk in it.

Then He put you into an environment that reaches into the deepest places in your soul and spirit. As you grow up and start to wake up to the thing for which you were called, you pick up your key. Since one key by itself isn't enough, you start to look around for another one. You're pretty sure that God must have it, and you become determined to catch up with Him.

The more you pursue Him, the closer you get. When it's time for your destiny to come to light, it will. The thrill of discovery is only going to be overshadowed by the thrill of fulfillment when you have finished the rest of the race of your life.

In any case, it's never too late. God's timing is perfect. He's never late. Believe He can show you your dream, and believe He can carry you through to its completion.

God Knows What He's Doing

Put your faith in the right place. Put it in God. He is the One who knows what He's doing.

You may look at your life right now and say, "Jentezen, I don't see much evidence of what you're talking about. I still have the same problems. I just cannot see the blessing in it."

Keep going. You are not the exception. He doesn't have any exceptions in His kingdom. God knows what He's doing with you. And He loves you. Your life right now may be in a time of "small beginnings." (See Zechariah 4:10.)

God knows what He's doing—all the time. He is faithful, and He will always do what He said He would do. Whether He has you in a wilderness time, a time of sowing, or a time of

*Y*our God will not let

you down. He can't. It would go

against His character to let you

down. Believe that you can

because you believe that He can.

You can depend on Him!

harvest, He's with you. He's the One who has the key to your heart and to your future.

> As time goes on, you will
> realize that your burden has
> become your passion.

When it's time for something to happen, He'll make sure it happens. God has a plan for you, and it's already in action right now.

Put Away Your Measuring Stick

Wherever you find yourself in the process, don't put limits on what God can do! He is infinite, and so are the possibilities for the dreams that He gives people. The trouble is, we have a very strong tendency to put limits on Him, especially when it comes to our dreams and visions for our lives. We think we are the final authority on our lives and that we know what's best and what's realistic.

> Believe that you can
> because you believe that He can.
> You can depend on Him!

Be careful that you don't end up trying to stand against God just because you think you know what you're doing. God Himself doesn't want you to keep measuring yourself or your circumstances against your idea of reality.

> I lifted up mine eyes again, and looked, and behold a man with a measuring line in his hand...And, behold, the angel that talked with me went forth, and another angel went out to meet him.
>
> —*Zechariah 2:1, 3*

See the picture in your mind. There was a young man who took a measuring line because he was going to try to measure what God was doing in the city of Jerusalem. God was disturbed by that. He was disturbed enough to dispatch an angel from heaven on the spot to stop him. And when the angel said to the young man, "Son, what are you doing?" and the man said that he was going to measure the width, breadth, and height of Jerusalem, the angel said back to him, "Put your measuring line away, son, because anything that God is involved in is unmeasurable."

God didn't want anybody to put limits
on what He could or would do.

God didn't want anybody to put limits on what He could or would do. God knew that as soon as people started measuring the city, they would define the boundaries, and they would box God in. Their measurements would make a statement about what they felt God is capable of.

Instead of believing that we can accomplish what God gives us to do, we put limits on everything. In theory, we may believe that God can accomplish the impossible, but in practice, we draw boundaries.

God says, "I'm going to use you," and your first response is, "But I come from the bad side of town. I don't have any education. My daddy left my family when I was a kid. I've got so many handicaps..."

Don't you think your response should be more like Mary's response? The angel told her that she would become pregnant even though she was a virgin and that she would bear the Son of God. She was startled, but she didn't object to the Word (Luke 1:34, 38). No ifs, ands or buts. She didn't put any limits on her unlimited God.

Pharisee Measuring Sticks

It's as if we have a "Pharisee spirit" in us. I say that because in Jesus' day, the Pharisees were the professional "measurers."

God may say to you, "I've anointed your son to serve Me in a special way." But immediately you take your measuring line

ou need to stop

measuring your earning capacity

by what you earned last year or

by your previous achievements in

the working world. That just puts

a cap on what God can do.

and hold it up against your son and read the markings on it. It doesn't have markings in inches. Instead, the markings read things like, "learning disorder," "not college material," and "not interested in God." So we measure him and find him deficient—in our estimation. As a result, we throw out the Word of the Lord without even really considering it.

The Pharisee spirit likes to hang around churches. It likes to pull out the religious tape measure and walk around measuring people, saying, "That's a nice suit of clothes. But you used to be a drug addict, didn't you? I heard that you're divorced. I won't expect much from you."

I know you've done that kind of thing, because I've done it myself. We've all done it, and we've all had it done to us. The only concept of measurement you need is one of God's infinite ability and capability. God's call will supersede everything else in your life. He is unmeasurable, and so is everything He does.

Unlimited Supply

Some of you have looked at your bills recently. And then you looked at your paycheck, and it wasn't enough to pay them. Out came your old measuring tape, and you said, as the disciples said before the Lord multiplied a few loaves and fish to feed five thousand-plus people, "What are they among so many?" (John 6:9). Your version is, "See, what is so little income with so many bills? Even if I had two jobs, it wouldn't be enough."

The only concept of measurement you need is one of God's infinite ability and capability.

That's a tape-measure mentality in action. Over against our limited version of the possibilities, we have God. God has a "maximum mentality." You need to stop applying your minimum mentality with your maximum God.

He is a God of increase. He is a God of abundance. With Him, if we will only give Him what we have and trust Him with it, and begin to obey Him when He tells us what to do, we will start to see increase.

Don't Measure Yourself Out of a Miracle

Don't let yourself get influenced by the people around you who say, "God might be strong enough to do anything, but I don't think He's doing those kinds of things today."

Don't hinder the miraculous from happening in your life. Don't be like the Israelites who should have known better because they had experienced so many miracles, but they went ahead and said, "Can God furnish a table in the wilderness?" (Ps. 78:19).

Sure, they didn't have any food in sight. And they were genuinely worried about starving to death. But that shouldn't have made them conclude that God was too limited to help them.

God could—and did—provide for them. He was bigger than famine and thirst then, and He still is today.

Much More Than Ankle Deep

We can find another "measuring line" in Ezekiel 40:1–5. The man (or angel) took Ezekiel on a complete tour of the temple and its courtyards, measuring everything in sight with his measuring rod. Then, when they came to the eastern gate, where water was gushing out and flowing down away from the temple, they waded in, and the man began to measure the depth of the water.

Notice that as long as they kept measuring, they could only get ankle deep, knee deep and waist deep. After they waded in up to their waists, it got too deep to walk in; it was a river. They couldn't measure the river. It was deep and wide, and its banks were lush with fruit trees. That river was unlimited, full of life and blessing.

If you accept your
own assigned playing field,
nobody can limit your success.

That's a picture of our life in the Lord—unlimited in blessing, unmeasurable. If you put away your measuring lines, tapes and rods and just let the Son of God show you where He wants you to go, you will soon forget about boundaries and limits.

The potential of your dream is tremendous. If you accept your own assigned playing field, nobody can limit your success. God is the One who decides how "successful" you will be, because no matter who plants and sows and tills the soil, it is God who gives the increase (1 Cor. 3:7). You can't make your own seed grow any more than you can make the sun shine. Your life is in His hands.

Unlimited!

Once you've had increase in your life, you will be able to recognize that it wasn't your brilliance that did it. It was God's doing. He could have left you back in your field as a sower. All your life you could have kept sowing and resowing the seed. But He gave the increase, and now you can see the whole picture.

Let your dream live, and let it flow! You can flow with it. God wants you to grab hold of your dream so that at the end of your life on Earth, you can say with the apostle Paul, "I was not disobedient unto the heavenly vision" (Acts 26:19). Put away your measuring line, and let God take you to meet your destiny.

Believe that you can! "For with God nothing shall be impossible" (Luke 1:37)!

Taking Hold:

- God knows what He's doing. When it's time for something to happen, He'll make sure it happens, whether it happens slow or fast.
- Put away your measuring stick. There is absolutely no limit to what your God can do!

JENTEZEN FRANKLIN

is the pastor of Free Chapel in Gainesville, Georgia,
and Orange County, California. He resides in Georgia
with his wife, Cherise, and their five wonderful children.
He is the author of *Believe That You Can*, *Fear Fighters*,
and the *New York Times* best seller *Fasting*.

For more information about Jentezen Franklin
and his ministries, visit
www.jentezenfranklin.org

For more info on Charisma House, visit
www.charismahouse.com
www.facebook.com/charismahouse